The Digital Nature of Man

On the limits between organic and digital lives

Digital Nature of Man

ISBN: 9798512367971

Dedication

The birds are singing under the windows of death. Should we silence them to respect death, or let them sing to respect life?

The birds are singing under the windows of death. I would nevertheless wish they sing elsewhere this morning. Let them not be under my mother's windows. The one who carried me must now be extinguished. A tragedy is being written. Apart from past stories, what will remain? Her memories will fade away and only mine will remain.

The walls, the things, the objects, will also remain, immutable. These things, which have not changed, cruelly make us forget momentarily our loss. Or they haunt us with fragile images of the past.

People seem to have already forgotten what she was like. The person at the center of my world has gone, and they don't care?

Overtaken, a part of my universe has collapsed, but the new day dawns all the same. So, I can do nothing but listen. Listen to the birds sing. They will always remind me of the love my mother had for them. The love I had for my mother.

I dedicate this work

To my mother,
and the birds.

Preface

A preface is not intended to summarize a book. Like all good authors, Charles Perez does not fail, both on the back cover and at the end of each chapter, to put his words together. I would only do a very clumsy educational exercise that the author does very well at the end of each section. I note, though not a specialist in the multiple domains, the level of erudition of this book, precise and ample scholarship which he testifies. Through the investigation of research, theories, achievements, innovations, creations of what can be condensed in the expression of digital technologies, the author is in search of what a human being is. Over the fifty-five chapters, divided into four sections, each short and lucid, capturing the attention, Charles Perez takes us through problems like order and disorder, language and words, space and time, movement and change, knowledge and ignorance, the arts and creation, often with the help of authors or myths of antiquity. As technical as the presentations are, with a multitude of concepts or terminologies that can lose the uninitiated reader, we can see the philosophical depth of the work.

What caught my interest the most, and which is not very frequent among the many authors who tell us about the upheavals that the sciences produce in all our established or traditional representations, especially in their conjunction, is the fact that we have entered a new era where there is no longer the human and his culture facing nature, but a hybridization. Life forms can be or become technological, and vice versa, as humans form new units and new contracts with other living beings. This entry into a history that we could not predict, by the very fact that we do not know where we are going refutes transhumanism, which claims to lead the destiny of humans towards a transformation that can go as far as immortality. I have spent my life associating with so-called disabled people and studying their history, and I know how technology can reduce their impairments and increase their capacities. The figure of Oscar Pistorius, before he became an assassin, is emblematic and symbolic. But I learned that strength can only be understood in relation to weakness. The extreme of strength turns into weakness just as the extreme of weakness can lead to a form of tyranny. Our limits make us what we are: human beings. If we want to deny any limits, starting with that of death, we are destroying what we cannot renounce: freedom. The false promise of transhumanism, not to be confused with what might be called the post or dis-humanism - as a form of classical humanism has probably done its time - entering under the pretext of science, as new forms of totalitarianism

Charles Perez, finally, brings us back to the simplicity of his garden. We must come back to earth, in all his new compositions, so that it remains our earth.

Henri-Jacques Stiker
Philosopher, anthropologist

"Today's history is already seeing, now, all the seductions of artificial intelligence and transhumanism on the agenda in the more or less near future. What, for better or for worse, will dominate this future era even more than ours is science."

An endless hosanna
Jean d'Ormesson

Preamble

Digital technologies are rewriting our history, our society, our future and certainly one day they will rewrite life. A life that finds its way without too many constraints in the two worlds (digital and organic) with such ease and speed that it seemed important to me to trace, at least partially, its path, its impact. As I walked through the two spaces and species of progress, I was surprised, amazed and worried. The level of fascination that the universe provokes/create in us is proportional to its level of improbability. In this improbable space, man has offered us knowledge that has transcended itself for several decades. Physics (quantum in particular), genetic engineering, computer science, robotics, artificial intelligence are vectors of exceptional progress.

Life is digitalized, like the Caenorhabditis Elegans: a small worm whose neural network's complexity (the connectome) is now totally under control, and which can be fully simulated on a computer. From neural activation to behavior, we know almost everything about this tiny life form of just over a millimeter. The organic connects to the digital with or without wires, but always by opening new avenues.

Men control insects with electrical impulses to make them run in the direction men wish.

Men rewrite the genetic codes of life to simplify, arrange or synthesize it. Others are working to create a general artificial intelligence capable, at least, of equaling us.

Men create new arts and new works, relying on algorithms, nature, mathematics. A nature that even blows us musical scores. And genetically modified bacteria recite our poems.

Finally, men are struggling with the well-known disease of old age. Others have dreams of immortality.

The great book of nature has never revealed so many secrets and mysteries to us. Technology and science have offered us a new way of reading it, of drawing inspiration from it. We even observe a new desire to write our stories, our story in new pages of this book.

It was already unimaginable and incomprehensible that our sciences are inspired, nourished and represent the reflections of nature, reality and our universe as well. It is even more surprising to observe man playing with this new power of knowledge and technicality today: to the point of allowing him to replay certain scenarios, to reverse certain effects of nature, and to surpass himself in many areas. To the point of creating machines that exceed man himself, and perhaps even one day technologies that will allow him to shed his body to change his envelope.

This fiction, but also this new reality, is more and more perceptible. We have the duty to measure it, to control it and to protect (it from) what we are. Little by little, behind a machine, we have enabled so many of us evolve. This new reality is perceived and offers us a mystery that must be understood and learned. A new reality that calls into question many of our beliefs and our certainties. These shape our objects, our stories, and our perception of truth differently. To illustrate this, we will deal with art, nature, knowledge, and death; facets of our life/cultures to which man has always been attached to as landmarks, stars, or even a spiritual guide; facets that move and move, that appear and disappear.

This book presents the outlines of what the direction taken by humans towards a digital nature looks like, observed, and inspired by recent and atypical creations. A digital nature inspired by recently exceeded limits. We will wonder about the place of man and our common future. An incentive to think about the future and to philosophize about it with a single goal, to build a future compatible with humanisme.

This non-fictional novel investigates the place of man alongside nature, to the universe, to his fate. It deepens this look into man's relationship to knowledge and creation. It advances until our scheduled end. Throughout this story, we will investigate the place of technology and the machine. They have overturned pillars dating back millennia of evolution, while being inspired by natural work. Where are we going? Who are we? What are we going to become? What is this strange power that has just entered human hands?

Introduction

Mankind has reached a crucial point in its development, in its history. It occupies a place that is almost anecdotal in the universe, but also one of the most fascinating and unique. From a universe of nearly 13.8 billion years to human beings (homo *sapiens)* who appeared only 300,000 years ago. Man is the luckiest and most improbable result of an organization of matter and the effect of time. An organization that enabled life to develop from a primary form to a sophisticated and intelligent form.

At this point in our development, it is impossible to ignore the impact of the technologies that are in our hands. Already in 2012, the CIA (Central Intelligence Agency) and the National Intelligence Council presented a vision of the world in 2035. The proposed landscape is largely imbued with a transhumanist tendency. There Man is imagined as being improved by more and more artefacts, prostheses and sensors of all kinds. Brain implants are being considered. The expectation is that technological man could evolve considerably in the coming decades.

Note carefully that if this technology has allowed us to rise, it has sometimes reduced us, even to the point of making us slaves. If man has always been a prisoner of time, today he is in an ambiguous position of strength and weakness. He is weakened by tools that go beyond his measure, weakened by a climate emergency, weakened by the latest health crisis.

Faced with a catastrophic situation swept away by an almost irreversible modification of the biosphere, of the planet, our current ability/capacity to self-destruct, technologies are also able to provide solutions and also a source of change in our own humanity.

Neuroscientist Demis Hassabis, who in 2010 was also founder of *DeepMind Technologies Limited* in 2010 (sold to Google in 2014), says that without the emergence of disruptive technologies, humans would certainly have a lot of worries about their own future. Artificial intelligence in particular (the machine's ability to reproduce traits of human intelligence) carries this hope. We can then understand why Rico Malvar, the scientific director of the Microsoft laboratory, compared the advent of artificial intelligence to that of electricity: a resource on which both machine and man are dependent.

Other specialists go further and stipulate a rupture possibly as strong as that implied by writing. In this line of superlatives, current Google president Sundar Pichai compares the importance of artificial intelligence with that of the discovery and domestication of fire. The symbol is strong. Fire is at the origin of the significant advance of man, it is the promise of being able to provide a rich and varied diet, the promise of heat and that of being able to create tools, and, later, machines. A fire which, in many mythologies, would have been obtained by man by stealing it from the gods. In Greek mythology, Prometheus (Προμηθεὺς) discreetly steals the celestial fire. Fire that he will obtain by concealing a torch lit in the sun and hidden under a bushel of fennel (Figure 1). Will the fire of artificial intelligence also bring a new phase of our civilization? A fire stolen from the gods or by men who approach and think they are gods? Keep in mind that this stolen fire led to torture. Prometheus was dragged by Zeus (Ζεὺς) to the Caucasus Mountains and was chained to a rock, where every day his liver will be eaten by an eagle, where every day his liver will grow again. Legend allows Prometheus to survive thanks to the savior Heracles.

 Will we be entitled to such a rescue in our quest? By laying the foundations of an intelligence and soon perhaps of consciousness in machines, isn't man touching on something divine and destructive?

We are observing the signs and the promise of a new era brought about by the convergences of technologies and advances in various fields, even to the point of rethinking the nature of man who now evolves in a space that can be described as 'hybrid'. Milad Doueihi mentions the hybridization "of our habitable space, our modes of communication and our modes of identity ". Hybridization driven by artificial intelligence, the web, Internet of Things, cloud computing (*cloud*), mass data (*big data*), robotics, UAVs, genetic engineering, nanotechnology and biotechnology. An evolution of our species which was already highlighted in 1960 by the philosopher Herbert Marshall McLuhan [6] with regard to the impact of media and technologies. He explains this change to us: "During the mechanical ages, we had extended our bodies in space. Today, after more than a century of electrical technology, we have extended our central nervous system into a global embrace, abolishing both space and time with respect to our planet. Quickly we enter the final phase of human extensions - the technological simulation of consciousness, when the process of creating knowledge will collectively and corporately be extended to the whole of human society, just as we have already extended our senses and our nerves by the various media."

Figure 1 : Work by Heinrich Friedrich Füger " Prometheus presents fire to humanity ", 1817.

In the XX1st century, Man has the possibility of forming a hybrid of his flesh by combining it with digital technologies. We are now moving towards an era where physical and digital will no longer stand separately. We envision a major anthropological revolution, often combined with hope of an intelligent society, although the uncertainty remains.

Is our very existence doomed to see organic nature converge with digital nature, thus redefining the contours of the new digital nature of man?

Bits, Atoms, Neurons and Genes

BANG!

We refer to the expression *Little Bang,* as opposed to the *Big Bang* of the creation of the universe. This cosmic event which saw a tiny point of gigantic density and heat become the source of our entire universe. Tomorrow, from person-machine interfaces, *phygital,* virtual or alternative reality, general artificial intelligence, up to intelligent dust could disrupt customs that are hundreds of thousands of years old. We are moving towards a new bang, symbol of a new creation, of a new beginning.

Electricity, Writing, Fire, Big Bang.

As you will have understood, this digital life follows the footsteps of our evolution. Little by little, it goes beyond the frontiers that stood before it. Man is rewriting his history through technology. The comparisons are strong, almost as big as our ambition.

Many scientists have the same feeling, that of belonging to a pivotal generation and at the foot of an Everest of gigantic developments. The signals alert us, progress indicates it: dazzling advances will be offered to future generations. Literary critic Nancy Katherine Hayles made an impression as early as 1999 when she claimed that man had somehow already merged with technology. She points out that all current forms of technology are so ubiquitous that they act on us as a reflection of the image of our actions on it.. We are up against the wall. A progress wall or a prison wall: we do not know which. If, throughout history, the future has never ceased to be uncertain, ours seems to bear even more uncertainties. We had not envisioned a man on the moon or a horse full of men in Troy. We didn't want to believe that colored men were equal to others. We have known many civilizations which which seemed eternal, only to collapse into dust and ashes, as a renewal and an eternal repetition of our works and our mistakes. We have believed that those who mastered the past had a more accurate view of the future.

Before a man decodes the code of life.
Before another creates an artificial cell.
Before we have fun reviving an extinct species.
Before we lengthen the ends of our telomeres to gain a little life.
Before we imagine and realize quantum computers capable of calculating at the scale of the particle.
Before we understand that the information of matter can be transmitted instantaneously to two places in space.

Before we create thinking machines and start to want to give them a
consciousness.
Before ...

Today, more than ever, everything seems possible. Yet, as our progress
shakes our way, we have never been so uncertain of our future.

Man feels strong in all his progress, all his discoveries, all his
exploits. Nevertheless, he is obviously all the more fragile. A superhuman can
quickly fall, mythology has given us many examples. A life of immortality
could turn out to be much drier and more agonizing than a mere mortal
life. The gift offered to Midas (Μίδας), that of turning everything he touched
into gold, turned into a handicap that could have been fatal. The myth
informs us that "Midas was surrounded by gold: the vases, the tables and the
chairs, but also the trees and the fruits... everything was transformed,
everything had the same color, the same touch. Midas could no longer taste
food, he could no longer quench his thirst. Desperate, Midas begged
Dionysos (Διώνυσος) to withdraw this gift from him. Then the god ordered
the king to dive into the Pactolus River, and the strange power of Midas
vanished. But, since then, the water of the Pactole is charged with a multitude
of gold spangles. "

In this mad ambition, and as long as we do not have a setback, worries come
face to face with fascination. How lucky we are to live at this time! What a
joy to understand so much, and to have so many ambitions! Millennia
working in a world of common sense on the rather banal scale of man,
without miniature, without gigantism. Man has now offered himself the
knowledge of the small, and even of the very small. He offered himself the
knowledge of the great and the far, and even the very great and the infinitely
far. We have ceased to dream with everyday objects of everyday desires. We
have offered ourselves a road to the wisdom (or insanity) of a more universal
knowledge. It inspires all men, the greatest as well as the humblest. We
continue to want, we continue to hope, but on scales without measures.

Man, almost has the power to rewrite man, to reinvent him, and technology
already has a lot to do with it. We can sense this moment in human history
as unique. Before this expected explosion of knowledge, of changes, of
dreams, of reality, learners, the living, artists, and immortals are inspired every
day.

In this work, we engage in a quest for the dimensions relating to what we will
call the digital nature of man. This nature can be perceived through
knowledge, art, life, and farewell, through little stories of what is part of our

great history. This universal history offers us a transdisciplinary look at humanity, a history where we still have a part of our destiny in our hands, a destiny that each of us can still write.

We begin our exploration with the inexhaustible question of knowledge and its relation to time. A question which, again, must be understood with a technological dimension.

Time passes, knowledge endures

Where it is a question of knowledge and its relation to time and technology.
We deal with what sums up the essential and its conservation.

"Equations are more important to me because politics is for the present,
but an equation is for eternity."
Albert Einstein

FIRST CHAPTER
The paradox of time and instability
Where the author draws a face of words in the paradox of time.

I am

The paradox of time

I don't know what formed me here

And what I'm doing here I don't know

Digging the earth, I go back in time

Looking at the sky, I go back in time

Opening a tree, I go back in time

Hatching eyes, the photons have aged

If everything in this world seems to have passed

What to seize from a present already picked

Barely written, immediately read

This verse belongs to the past

That however I will never go back up

What do we look like? Words engage me

When the data encodes me, words stare at me

And their memory returns memories to the present

Man is locked in a paradox of time where he seems, despite himself, to belong to a present which only offers him furtive images of the past. Memory opens a door to him and a hope for the future. He reigns seated during this constantly moving present. A symbol of instability carried by a changing environment, but also by its own evolution. This being changing by nature reflects a world that is changing around him every moment. Unknowingly drawn into the movement of this - not always - sacred boat of life, over time he observes a volatile landscape. Its reflection in water, air, fire, and earth will make it evolve. His journey constitutes the experience that grows in him. Even to the point that, at times, some of his thoughts are established as convictions and his experiences as memories.

Technologies would have surprising power. They would go so far as to create memories that we did not know. Memories lived by proxy through the images that we consult on the devices that accompany us. Memories that are not part of our history.

Man constantly fluctuates in the midst of beliefs and ideas that are created and fade, without sinking, in the midst of a world that is made and undone, and above all beyond us. These cells are dying, are created and multiply. They number in the billions in our organism and are in constant (re)organization. These billions of pixels that change our perceptions, these innumerable ideas written on a few things and often a little on everything. These words read, these words spoken, heard, these images perceived, memorized, and sometimes forgotten. What we are anchored in is a perpetual movement, in a world in perpetual revolution, carried by the stars, the planets, other humans and by its mirror. Unstable men, in an almost permanent instability and on all scales. The universe dictates this instability behind a grossly stable appearance. Everything revolves, everything moves and matter walks in a movement and an exchange of energy, in a multitude of references, and some spatial and temporal dimensions: spatiotemporal, we have been taught. At every scale, it vibrates, it is shocking, we interact, it disappears and appears, we live, and we die, we develop and collapse.

As a result of this instability, however stable, man, his emotions and his decisions can vanish or be created under the effect of an anecdotal reality. Psychologist and Nobel Laureate in Economics, Daniel Kahneman had highlighted one of our many flaws - new information can shift an acquired position and change a decision, a belief, and certainly a future in no time. In this sense, a part of what constitutes man is and will remain inconsistent, while science often offers us a semblance of consistency, precisely and often behind a cognitive unknown and far from being materialistic.

The sciences, soft or hard, become more flexible in the hands of man. If the Greek philosopher Heraclitus liked to say that no one bathes twice in the same river, the dry arms of the Nile remind us that the river does not always lie down in the same bed. Man will never bathe twice in the same reality nor in the same spirit, nor at the same time, the same present. More precisely, we should read: man never bathes twice in the same consciousness, in the same information. He will never walk twice with the same man. The spirit of the Amazon River sometimes comes out of its bed to offer us amazing images. Under certain climatic conditions, clouds form above its bed. These clouds draw a parallel aerial river which follows the course of the river. Part of it then seems to rise towards the heavens. It is a path that the digital man could follow.

CHAPTER II
Crossing time like others are crossing space
Where man can be inspired by a grain of sand and a particle.

Two elements as small as a grain of sand and a particle can transmit a dream to man: that of crossing space and time.

Earth has seen grains of sand fly over the oceans. It's not a metaphor, dust of sand from the Sahara Desert regularly crosses part of the Atlantic Ocean. Sailors are the first witnesses of this haze slender gray ribbons of gray, colored faintly yellow or red. It can appear in the middle of a sunny ocean. These mists of sand have been generated on the coast of Cape Verde, in several parts of the island, from beaches of clear sand. There's red and gold sand on a volcanic island that should only be surrounded by black sand beaches. A hardly believable epic, under the effect of the wind, a path is created between two coasts separated by nearly 600 kilometers.

We discover a description of this phenomenon in an old article by geographer Camille Vallaux published in the annales de géographie in 1930. "These mists mainly result from dust and fine sand from the desert which come from the neighboring coasts of the continent between Cape Juby and Cape Verde where the Saharan sands can reach the sea without the interposition of mountain ridges. Dust mists often intercept the view from a distance of 2 miles; the thickest, which, in cloudless skies, only show the midday sun like a red disc, are accompanied or followed by falling dust which covers the decks of the boats with a thin red layer. [...] It is the currents of height (from 1000 to 2000 meters) which transport them, the currents at ground level having rather the character of a monsoon from east to west. At the beginning and at the height of the summer, the mists and the dust falls diminish, without ever disappearing entirely." Satellites now offer us proof of this epic (Figure 2). A symbol that lets us believe in the power of wind and lightness alone.

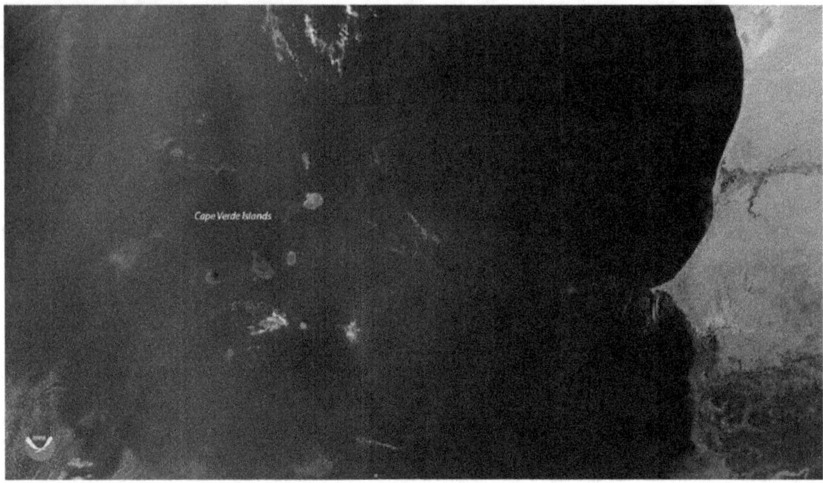

Figure 2 : On December 9, 2018, image captured by the NOAA-20 VIIRS instrument which scans the Earth twice a day at a resolution of 750 meters. NOAA credit.

Another adventure crosses space, that of information carried by entangled quantum particles or so-called twins. To understand it, we must observe the heart of matter, the infinitely small. Even though two twin particles (e.g., photons) are several kilometers apart, if one is changed, the other instantly changes into a dependent state. The information seems to be teleported into space without any real support. These particles are said to form a linked system. Linked, of course, but quite independent of their positions in space. This phenomenon seems promising for the future of communications. It was tested in 2007 with twin photons located in the Canary Islands. They were separated between La Palma and Tenerife. The quantum information carried by the photons then traveled 144 kilometers instantly.

Since then, a Chinese satellite has been able to transmit entangled photons to Earth at a distance of more than 1,000 kilometers. An absolute record and certainly also a promise of one day having a quantum internet. In the short term, we imagine a quantum cryptography allowing the exchange of encryption keys, by extension of messages, in a completely secure manner. This brick, making it possible to keep the secret of our digital telecommunications, would become unbreakable.

The public evokes the term quantum teleportation and more precisely quantum entanglement because there is no transport of matter. This property at the heart of the infinitely small is a source of reflection on the very meaning of our universe, of matter and of reality. Is quantum entanglement the ultimate natural resource? If we have said everything about artificial intelligence, we compare the quantum entanglement to the iron of our old Bronze Age.

To cross time, cross the ages, the possibilities are limited and so are the examples. The man is thrown into a snapshot of time, he does not resist it. Our planet holds a more than uncertain fate in its hands and our universe is perhaps the only one that does not have too much to worry about.

Man is a prisoner of a more than reduced space-time. However, it is this repository that allows him to open his eyes and discover the most beautiful things in the world. Often, it is about similar prisoners: animals, plants and other future vestiges, unconscious of their fate until the horizon of the events.

Fallen into the middle of everything that seems to us to be. Whether by mistake or by chance? Sometimes by a series of consequences whose logics don't seem (to us) too hard to master. For many others, for a reason for being so complex and incomprehensible that it all seems most simply: amazing. This space and this time exceed us as much as they carry us. What are the important questions? Our future, our future. Whatever the questions, they are carried by such limited knowledge, since we have only an instant of time, so present, and a point in space that makes everything beyond us. The only question will be: why do we have such a short existence, limited by a body that is so deeply grounded in this time and this space? Why this fortuitous form of human life? What is its primary meaning? To simply bring it back to man, to mankind seems a trap of simplicity to be avoided. What I understood is simple.

Everything is beyond me, and time flies.
No matter where I am, space flees from me.

In the history of humanity, with or without primary will, the creation of man is an object that defies at least time and space. This possibility is also offered by language, knowledge, our stories, and our myths These images make it possible to contemplate statues of Caesar, portraits of strangers, masks in Alaska, paintings in Malaga, vases in Greece, a whole set of Triumphal Arches and even ivory statuettes from the Paleolithic era. Some self-portraits also did not survive too badly, and our museums accompany them on this journey.

And some of our creations take the time of a breath without suffering too much.

Anthropologists know to what extent man knows how to forget time to make his creations and his stories survive. The Bhopas of Rajasthan have demonstrated an incredible ability to remember and recite poems thousands of lines long. Historian William Dalrymple has studied this phenomenon. Myths and legends pass through the ages and generations without too much modification. Sometimes with support, but often without support other than verbal transmission and the effort of memory. Our languages reflect this. They provide way to transcend the limits of our body and to afford an opportunity to belong to a past that is still alive. However, ! memory could perhaps one day seem like a luxury of conservation. I had an echo of a possible Atlantis, of a more reliable Colossus of Rhodes, of the library of Alexandria and of many marvels successively fallen into oblivion, as if stranded by time.

In a quest for stability and, as if to cross time and navigate space, man offered himself a quest, a power. This power is that of building a myth and a knowledge capable of enduring and of explaining what is most unthinkable in the world: life, time, the universe. In this quest to understand and create a resource to share, *homo sapiens* uses metaphors of different kinds. The first is scientific. The one that represents the world with figures, equations, models, symbolic creations. This metaphor is extraordinarily correct, which continues to surprise the greatest thinkers. However, it remains forever incomplete. The other more colorful and artistic is that of the myth. This myth carries with it a perceptible reality through culture and beliefs. The two images complement each other and offer man a wealth of interpretation and understanding of the world which has seduced scientists, philosophers, and artists through the ages.

CHAPTER III
Spiritual metaphors
Where science and mythology meet.

Are there more virtual artefacts in science than in mythologies and beliefs? Today's bosons, quarks, dark matter, the multiverse are no more perceptible realities for most of us than were Hercules, Zeus, Amon-Re or Shiva in previous ages.

Are our equations the right ones? Are the words right? I guess so, especially in the minds of those who build and use these things. All the same it is thanks to these empirical laws that we made important discoveries. Where the laws seemed to offer a perfect fit, we trusted in mathematics and calculations. Science has thus repeatedly imagined the existence of things that were until then unknown, invisible, inaccessible, and yet very real, often to reconcile laws, theory and observation. The Higgs boson is arguably the most famous and important example of recent years. Postulated in 1964 on a theoretical basis, the existence of the particle was validated experimentally in 2012. It is impossible to deny the simple fact that laws, words, metaphors undoubtedly have a real impact as soon as they take shape in our actions, our experiences, our knowledge, or our beliefs. They help us to get an idea of what surrounds us, of reality, of what makes up life, of what constitutes matter, universum, thought, and even consciousness.

Albert Einstein confessed: "I will always be amazed to see how mathematics, a pure product of the human imagination, corresponds so well to reality." Nevertheless, mathematics, like many sciences, has its weaknesses. Logician Kurt Gödel was to identify two of them within the framework of mathematical logic. He proved a first theorem stating that recursive systems of axioms contain at least one statement which cannot be proved or refuted. He added in a second theorem that a coherent theory does not demonstrate its own coherence. This limitation of the axiomatic method, even if it remains relatively minor, leaves room for questioning and uncertainty in a good number of arguments.

Scientific and spiritual realities are just pictures and metaphors of our world. More or less accurate metaphors, more or less harsh. Images useful for understanding it and for putting our knowledge, our lives and our society in order.

In a desire to organize heaven, the Babylonians identified the constellations more than 4000 years ago. At that period, they had in their sight the constellations of the northern hemisphere. Thus appeared the myths in the stars which occupy our sky: the lion, the scorpion, bison man, the old man, the fish. They gradually became linked with astronomy and history. From planets named after the Greek and Roman gods to constellations named after a winged horse (Pegasus) or a being half-man, half-horse (Centaur). The myth, in addition to being anchored in our cultures, is deeply anchored in the scientific reality of our stars. It is only later, after the great explorations, that we would name the constellations of the southern hemisphere discovered on that occasion. We would then assign them names related to navigation. They give us a double way of going back in time through light that took several thousands, millions and billions of years to reach us, but also as abstract images used to organize the sky. Constellations are thus the work of astronomers, navigators, explorers, and myths throughout history. A thread to reach the sky, which we owe to Ptolemy, Vespucci, Plancius, Keyser, Houtman, Hevelius, Lacaille and many others (see Figure 3 below).

The historian of science and technology, Adrienne Mayor, underlined the presence of questions about the place of man and machine from Greek mythology. Debates on the subject would have been initiated in ancient Greece. She points out the parallel as follows: " The question of what it meant to be human obsessed the ancient Greeks. Time and time again, their stories explored the promises and dangers of staving off death, expanding human capacities, reproducing life. The myths of Hercules, Jason and the Argonauts, the witch Medea, the engineer Daedalus, the inventor-god Hephaestus and the tragedy of Pandora raised the fundamental question of the boundaries between man and machine. "

New technologies have allowed a new form of myth to emerge. Digital mythology is present with fictional stories invented on the basis of digital works. Milad Doueihi speaks of a hybrid mythology between game and fiction. This is the case

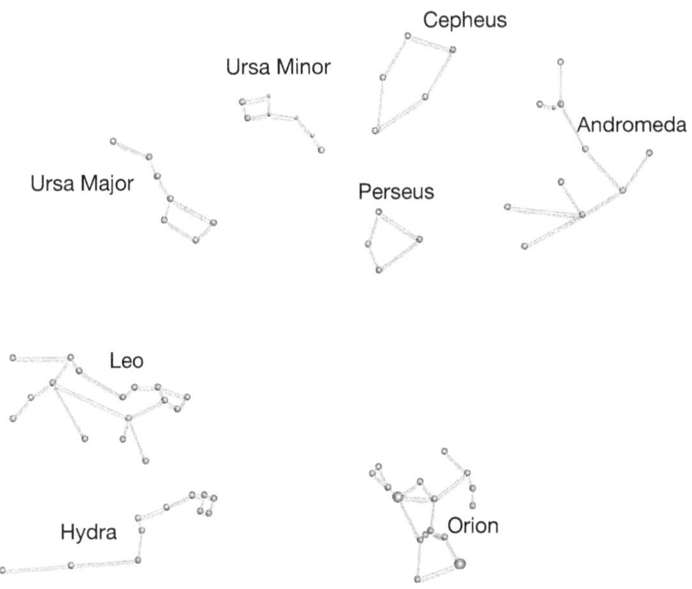

Figure 3 : Representation of some constellations of the celestial sphere.

of game characters whose stories and emotions are transcribed in books and myths. The Halo book series, for example, is at the intersection of two worlds. The same hybridity format exists with virtual influencers. These are digital computer models. Models of people whose physical appearance is perfectly anchored in social norms and canons of beauty. These men and women of synthesis are on social networks through their writings and their photos. The representations are mythical but carried by a character who seems quite real. Their audience follows these accounts en masse and even has a parasocial relationship with them. Lilmiquela has over 3 million Instagram followers. They are so convincing that some people speculate about the existence of a human being behind the avatar of these profiles, refusing to accept that they are simply an artificial creature.

Digital man has entered this new space of reality and abstraction which offers him a place of creativity and inspires him with new questions around fictional and artistic characters. Faced with the unknown and the strength of new virtual links, our digital myths have appeared. A symbol of the discovery of a new world that we do not yet fully understand but that we want to explain despite everything. The visible part of our artificial intelligences is observed with a worried and admiring eye. A return to a (another?) form of the intrigue of the world around us. The need to deify artificial characters, as we would have done with stars in another era. We respect and depend on them, but they are also entities that matter in our digital lives, and which are beyond us.

Myths are then images. A formal representation of an alternative explanation of the realm of reality. However, as sociologist Edgar Morin stated, phenomena cannot be dissociated from their representations. We must encode our reality under a formal representation in order to be able to manipulate it and finally decode it. A constructivist game mixing abstraction and reality that will always ask questions about the limits that can be reached in terms of truth. We think for example of Plato and the allegory of the cave.

Whether the abstraction is mathematical, mental, physical, mythological, or digital, it is reflected in the reality of men who bear it and transport it through time. Yet these metaphors are always fragile. How can order arise from disorder? How can knowledge be distorted and at times even erroneous?

CHAPTER IV
Of our very fragile worlds
Where worlds intertwine to offer us broken images of reality.

The 1st century Latin poet and philosopher, Lucretius, considered that a knowledge of nature should enable us to grasp the knowledge of reality; in contrast to the images and chimeras coming from our minds which is too often quick to believe in supernatural forces. Almost 2000 years later, in 1915, Michelis Enrico tells us that the most important step in modern criticism is to understand that a great part of divine and heroic myths are the result of historical reconstructions and explanations, thus giving reality a double image, perceived through different prisms of abstraction. Like light broken down into a sum of its colors or a sound into a sum of wave frequencies. Our reality is perceived through the mixtures of our representations. Which would finally clarify what it may have been from the start: a sensation?

Popol-Vuh teaches us, like all cultural histories of civilizations, the close link between belief and reality. In this fundamental text of the Maya-Quiché civilization, we discover traces of beliefs, and a myth about the origin of man. According to the writings, the gods would have liked to create creatures capable of paying homage to them, namely men. To do this, they would use earth and water, modeled into figurines in the image of a man with a head and a neck. This attempt was unsuccessful: these figurines dissolved under the effect of rainwater. However, they teach us important steps taken by the civilization of the time. They mark a period when the Mayas would begin working the land to create objects. These figurines and other earthen objects would give birth to pottery, then much later to ceramic works. A know-how that will subsequently spread widely. Raphaël Girard concluded that we are faced with an obvious and remarkable concordance between the information of Popol-Vuh and objective reality. One example among thousands of the subtle relationships between a culture, a belief, and a form of reality.

The sacred boat is one such image. In ancient Egypt, the boat reflects to what extent the life of the time was based on the wealth carried by the Nile (the

Nile was personified by the god Hâpy). It plays a preponderant role in belief. It is a symbol of the life, death, and resurrection of Osiris. The solar boat accompanies the souls of the dead to guide them towards the footsteps of the sun god. A symbol of a life held in this mythical object and whose imprint on Egyptian culture is preponderant. The peasants of the time had to take into account in the volumes of production the offerings to the gods. A belief anchored in actions, especially for this complex and arduous work on the land.

A myth told from generation to generation and carrying meaning on a daily basis would not have more impact on a civilization than historical facts, like multiplication tables learned by heart and without understanding. Trying to explain the meaning of the Battle of Marignan with a simple number is like a promise to forget the rest and banish the light of history behind a timeline. A mythical account of that moment would perhaps have marked our children more than a list of facts piled up without flavor, giving no taste or smell of the times.

Our physical space is itself an abstract object and a product of our spiritual conception. It seems difficult to come up with a suitable geometric model to understand this world. If space and Euclidean geometry have taught us a lot, they are not more present than other spaces and other geometries. Riemannian geometry (named after Bernhard Riemann) has taught us even more and made a broader look possible. Hilbert space has greatly informed our understanding of quantum mechanics. No geometry could offer a universality that would approach a perfect image of reality as a whole, or even of its space. The theory of superstrings (under its unified variant called theory M) teaches us that certain dimensions of space are folded up on themselves. Of the 11 dimensions of this theory, 7 are folded and one dimension remains: that of time. The folded dimensions are intangible on the scale of man, and yet, in a way, they exist. As a result, only our usual three dimensions remain observable. This tangible object that is space therefore seems to pose the same questions as time, the same problems. It hides mysteries whose effects we perceive, but whose cause and origin are difficult to understand fully. As soon as we dwell on it, the definitions of simple things no longer seem obvious, and a lingering doubt persists. "If no one asks me what time is, I know what it is; and if I am asked and I want to explain it, I no longer know it;" affirmed Saint Augustine in the 4th century. The sciences offer us projections of this space and this time, which by nature remains dependent on human representation as maintained by Immanuel Kant.

The metaphors of our world, whatever they are, are very fragile. A new scientific theory will perhaps one day erase a whole section of our knowledge with a stroke of genius and without warning. There would be a strange panic. This word, of Greek origin, comes directly from mythology. Pan (Πάν), the protector god of shepherds and pastures, half-man and half-goat, was able to terrorize travelers because of the abominable cries he emitted. Panic ensued.

The paradoxes of science show us both its weakness and its strength, its imprecision and its precision, its power, and its impotence. Étienne Klein dealt with the subject of the paradox. Here again, we are dealing with our inability to distinguish the real from its representation. He based his discourse on the paradoxes of physics, and in particular that of the reversibility of time.

Armed with this uncertainty, science forges a link with doubt via refutability. Any hypothesis, any theory must be refutable. It is thus, by construction, hypothetically true as long as it has not been demonstrated to be false. So be careful Remember, not long ago, The Earth was flat. It is round today. Yet the belief is not so obvious, and The Earth is still flat for some of us. They have a name, the platistes or terreplatistes. Generations obediently and diligently learned that Earth is at the center of the universe. We had, as proof for those who doubted it, maps corroborating with certainty this situation. The naturalist Charles Darwin suggested in 1871 the hypothesis of an origin of life in pools of hot water. He wrote "if we could conceive of a small, warm pond with all kinds of ammonia and phosphoric salts, light, heat, electricity, where a protein compound was formed chemically, ready to undergo even more complex changes, at present, this matter would be immediately devoured or absorbed, which would not have been the case before the formation of living creatures." This hypothesis is less certain with recent discoveries. They would indicate the possibility of a life form obtained from hydrothermal vents and underwater hydrothermal vents. The researchers conclude as follows: " The conditions not only allow the formation of protocols that initiate life, but actively promote it. "

We believed for a moment that the world was made of matter and ether. A substance that carried physics for a long time and which did not prevent many discoveries. The mathematician Henri Poincaré would affirm in 1902: "it does not matter whether the aether really exists, that is the business of metaphysicians. Today, the question of the aether seems totally outdated despite similarities to dark energy and the quantum vacuum." In its mythological origin, we already found the ether. Ether (Αιθήρ) was a primordial god of Greek mythology, his domain was that of the upper air. He therefore makes his domain an air breathed by the gods, in contrast to the air breathed by the simple mortals we are. It is interesting to note that in this mythology, it is time, Chronos (Χρόνος), which generates the ether. In our modern physical considerations on the origin of the universe, time is born with the Big Bang. Before, it didn't exist. There are many examples which need to be studied with vigilance and the dozens of theories on the origins of *homo sapiens* should also be taken with caution.

There are shocks between our multiple universal metaphors. At times throughout history, they are in disagreement, other times, they complement each other wonderfully. Does God play dice or not? Is there a great architect of the universe? What is behind reality? Behind conscience? What is the essential nature of reality? Perhaps a future civilization will write its beliefs, mythology, and history differently. Digital civilization will write it with new artefacts, and through an alterative reality, or one discovered differently than by our screens, our tools, our new objects, and our new species.

Our metaphors enrich our mind and our knowledge in their own way, two great pillars of progress. If they allow us to build buildings and artifacts, let us keep in mind their fragility. One of the purest symbols of this question has been preserved with simple and yet such true words. The writer, poet, and aviator, Antoine de Saint-Exupéry reminded us of that adults love numbers. "When you tell them about a new friend, they never ask you about the essentials. They never say to you: What is the sound of his voice? What are his favorite games? Does he collect butterflies? They ask you: How old is he? How many brothers does he have? How much does he weigh? How much does his father earn? Only then do they think they know him. So, if you tell them: The proof that the little prince existed is that he was lovely, that he laughed, and that he wanted a sheep. When you want a sheep, it's proof that you exist; they'll shrug their shoulders and call you a child! But if you tell them: the planet it came from is asteroid B 612 then they will be convinced, and they will leave you alone with their questions. They are like that. You should not blame them. Children should be very forgiving of grown-ups."

Should you keep your child's soul to understand the world? Is there a reality elsewhere than in our laws and in our numbers? Even if all the novels in the world have tried to convince us of this, there is still doubt.

By sweeping aside the metaphors available to man to extract the meaning of what surrounds him, we see under multiple abstractions and on many scales that there is a surprising link between order and disorder. This living paradox is also found in our new digital technologies.

CHAPTER V
An apparent disorder that hides an order
Where disorder weaves a subtle link with order.

Along with the question of images of reality arises the question of a historical paradox in our observations of nature - that of the order of things. In particular, it is a question of explaining how an apparent disorder can be at the origin of the order that we observe or seem to observe.

Greek mythology relates different versions of the creation of the world, what is called cosmogony. However, most versions agree on one fact, that of an origin in Chaos (Χάος). From unorganized matter, a form of order will be born. The appearance of the gods and all the other forces in the universe came after the chaos. If the myth does not converge with the idea of the Big Bang, it still offers an approach to and an image of the question. How can order arise from disorder? And more recently, how are our intelligent systems inspired by it?

The biologist and philosopher Henri Atlan summarized his observations by highlighting the importance of noise. Noise would be one of the secret ingredients allowing disorder to organize itself. He sums up the idea as follows: "The principle of complexity by noise, that is to say the idea of a positive effect noise, is the roundabout way we have of introducing effects of meaning, of signification, in a quantitative theory of organization. The origin of the universe, of life, of species, of systems of all kinds seem to be associated with this paradox of order and disorder to which we occasionally add a pinch of noise, of chance." The order observed is related to the surprising success of our abstract models to model the reality. Albert Einstein underlined the incredible order observed by man: "The human mind is not capable of understanding the Universe. We are like a little child entering a huge library. The walls are covered up to the ceilings with books in various languages. The child knows that someone must have written these books. He doesn't know who or how. He does not understand the language in which they are written. But the child notices a precise plan in the arrangement of the books. A mysterious order that he doesn't understand, but only vaguely suspects." The physicist Albert-László Barabási admits that the book of nature is hopelessly complex and remains the major challenge for the science of 21st century. "From society, a collection of seven billion people, to the communication systems, which today connect billions of devices, from computers to cell phones. Our very existence is rooted in the ability of thousands of genes to work together seamlessly: our thoughts, reasoning, and understanding of the world are hidden in the connections between the billions of neurons in our brains. These seemingly random systems, upon close inspection, display endless signatures of order and self-organization, the quantification, understanding, prediction, and possibly control of which are a major intellectual challenge."

This challenge has occupied the sum of the work of men of all ages. Science has thus opened this book in small steps and over time. Little by little, nature has opened up its secrets to us. The famous philosopher Pythagoras was one of the first to open a page with mathematics. At the time, and for one of the first times, he had equated the musical reality of our physical world. It establishes the relationship between the sound emitted by a string and its length. A passion carried by music and its meaning. This harmony of nature by numbers, or vice versa. A clue going in the direction of a beauty obtained by the order hidden in nature. "First, he attached corresponding weights to strings and heard their consonances by ear; then he applied double, median, or other proportions to pipe lengths, and conceived perfect assurance in his various experiments. Measuring them, he poured quantities of water corresponding by weight into glasses; and he struck these glasses, arranged according to the different weights, with a brass or iron stick, rejoicing to note that, there too, nothing diverged. Thus led, he turned to compare them to the length and thickness of the ropes. This is how he found the rule that is the monochord, in the double sense of the standard and the wooden measuring instrument [...] This type of rule gives such a fixed and firm vision that no one, among those who seek, can be misled... " [21].

Ideally, the discovery of laws in nature is without approximation and hypothetically without errors. In a way, these laws aim for perfection. Knowledge is intended to be universal and, if possible, without cultural ties. It must be fair to all as an indisputable reflection of reality. However, on closer inspection, it is easy to discover that errors are indeed present, and on multiple scales. They are even at the heart of the creation of life and knowledge. In fact, they even hold a creative power: to perfect and adjust one's work to the fairest, which coincides with our greatest happiness with the most beautiful.

CHAPTER VI
From disorder and errors to creative powers
Of the place of error in creation.

As soon as man tries to create or seize knowledge, if he wishes to transmit it, without having much choice, he must exchange it, write it and, in order to train, transform it, distort it. The history of myths is not exempt from this observation, and they evolve over time and transmission. They are content with modifications to the image of a culture, of a civilization.

Man makes mistakes. These mistakes are sometimes picked up and taken for granted. Are these dangerous or creative? I remember a book containing all the errors transmitted in our scientific educational books. A striking example was that of a diagram showing a barrel pierced in three places and from which the learners had to understand the relationship between the height and the pressure of a fluid: the principle of Evangelista Torricelli. The square of the flow velocity of a fluid under the effect of gravity is proportional to the height of the fluid located above the opening through which it escapes from the cylinder. A law of nature among millions of others. The illustration used almost systematically in school textbooks aimed to show that the lower the hole, the greater the flow velocity. The latter was a false simplification showing that the lowest water jet went further. History states that even Leonardo da Vinci had illustrated an imperfect picture of it. The pierced barrel made it easier to understand, but whoever tried the experiment understood the error. A jet near the base of the barrel hits the ground on which it is resting faster. The middle jet being the one that will go the furthest. This is explained not only by the pressure but by the distance of each hole from the table.

As soon as man enters the fountain of knowledge, he, who is its fundamental actor, tries to transmit elements of truth and makes mistakes, learns by mistake.

Looking at knowledge, only a few scientists had been its spokespersons for centuries and millennia. A paradigm that has evolved drastically with new technologies, new media and in particular the social and collaborative web. Before the establishment of a verification system, the information available on the digital encyclopedia Wikipedia was also unreliable. Today, that encyclopedia is the reflection of the best that man can do in the common creation of knowledge. As long as he takes the time, gets organized, adjusts, learns and corrects his mistakes. Wikipedias quality is good today. This has required more than 15 years of work, 15 years of self-organization. A work built by men who number in millions in historical contrast with *the Encyclopedia or the Reasoned Dictionary of Sciences, Arts and Crafts,* edited by a small circle (about 300 people) and which required more than 21 years of work. The project led by Denis Diderot and Jean Le Rond d'Alembert included a total of 60,000 entries, Wikipedia proudly sports more than two billion articles. For the French section alone, more than 20,000 active contributors have been identified.

Beyond this work, our digital instantaneous platforms raise a few issues. Digital technologies amplify mistakes, repeat them, and everyone can venture to convey their own version of the truth. The latter can be accepted by everyone, even if it is a false truth or a false information. A reflection of the dangerous new games mixing information and truth. Belief groups can be formed in our digital communities, like echo chambers. Sound boxes where individuals corroborate an unverified fact, none of whom have access to truthful information to deny it. In such cold rooms, Internet users mistakenly think they have the truth. False beliefs are magnified there, like an echo distorted by the slopes of our mountains. Digital technology offers us errors that are more complex to grasp and control. They are sometimes involuntary, everyone makes them, all the time. Think about blogs, billions of YouTube videos and billions of websites!

Far from the memory of water, mistakes can be good. A word deliberately flayed, a broken rhythm like Louis Aragon's. A trip to China and Japan by which Christopher Columbus discovers America for us. Iodine discovered by Bernard Courtois in the ashes of seaweed. Radioactivity by Henri Becquerel. The post-it too, we owe it to an error.

Nature makes mistakes like man, who is a miraculous product. He had time to acquire a genetic heritage which has known many epics. Epics which led to a life form of incredible complexity and ingenuity. So, let's be vigilant, we may have made the mistake of manipulating living DNA. Do these errors hide other ambitions, such as chance and necessity and sometimes also spontaneity. Man emerged from nothingness, from the Big Bang, from the living, from a common ancestor. Was this possible without appealing to some form of chance and error? The famous Greek materialist philosopher Democritus claimed that everything in the universe is the result of chance and necessity. Remarks highlighted by the Nobel Prize for physiology Jacques Monod, in particular with regard to biology. Laws are a strong symbol of our reading of the ledger. However, there is still a doubt about the place of chance in the expression and emergence of these laws. Physicist Stephen Hawking added: " We cannot make nucleic acids in the laboratory from non-living materials. But given 500 million years ago and the oceans covering most of the Earth, there could be a reasonable probability that RNA was made by chance. As the DNA reproduced itself, there would have been random errors, many of which were harmful and disappeared. Some would have been neutral - they would not have affected the function of the gene. And some errors would have been favorable to the survival of the species - these would have been chosen by Darwinian natural selection."

Injecting a dose of chance is therefore often a saving grace for our biological, mechanical and even artificial systems. Mistakes are at the heart of our processes, and the one who no longer commits mistakes must resolve to destroy his learning by destroying himself. Entrepreneur Bill Gates once said that success is a bad teacher. It makes smart people believe they are infallible. The American statesman and the twenty-sixth president of the United States, Theodore Roosevelt taught us: "The only man who never makes mistakes is the one who never does nothing."

Life is a symbol here. It is constantly in search of reproduction, division, action and reaction. His quest never ends and encompasses a mechanic that makes mistakes and learns from mistakes. She even seems to know how to deal with most of her mistakes over time. A talent that we unfortunately do not always have.

Our most impressive artificial intelligences learn from their failures. This is how, little by little, the machine was able to surpass human performance. As early as 2015, *Deep Mind* artificial intelligence had demonstrated learning faculties allowing it to adapt to tasks of various kinds. It has, for example, reached a level of human excellence on many games of the Atari 2600 console. The researchers specify this advance as follows [25] : "This work bridges the gap between high dimensional sensory input and actions, resulting in the first artificial agent capable of learning to excel at a wide range of difficult tasks."

Generative antagonist networks are algorithms capable of self-programming in the image of nature. In this model, two networks clash: a generator and a discriminator. The first generates an artificial image and the second tries to predict whether this image is artificial or synthetic. This competition between the networks makes it possible to obtain the synthesis of extremely realistic images. The machine wins by fighting itself and keeping its best versions to face each other again. An almost Darwinian success loop that reaches new heights. This self-organization of the neural network closely resembles the capacity observed in nature. Most of our predictive models come close to errors. They do not systematically seek to cancel them but weave a tight bond with them. They must understand that mistakes are a mark of adaptability, a guarantee of success.

In a model without errors, the risk is great.
The risk of having understood a little too well a reality that faces us by obscuring a reality that we ignore.

A lesson understood by the man in his early attempts to measure where perfection is impossible, and where an error margin should be tamed. This reality is materialized by the famous curves bearing the name of Friedrich Gauss (bell curves), which are widely found in nature, and which initially bore the name of the law of errors. The observation is intuitive, but profound: small errors occur more often than large ones.

We wish to give our artificial models a form of universality in order to offer them a transversal use. There is therefore a balance to be found between an over-trained and under-trained model. We speak on one hand of under-learning, and on the other of over-learning. These images are objects of reflection for our pedagogy. To allow it a longer lifespan, we will favor a program that is tolerant to imperfections, more adaptable and more robust to minute changes.

A few noise elements integrated into an image are enough to fool our pattern recognition algorithms (those of *deep learning* - deep learning). Just add a tiny noise to the image on the left for the system to mistake a panda for a gibbon (Figure 4).

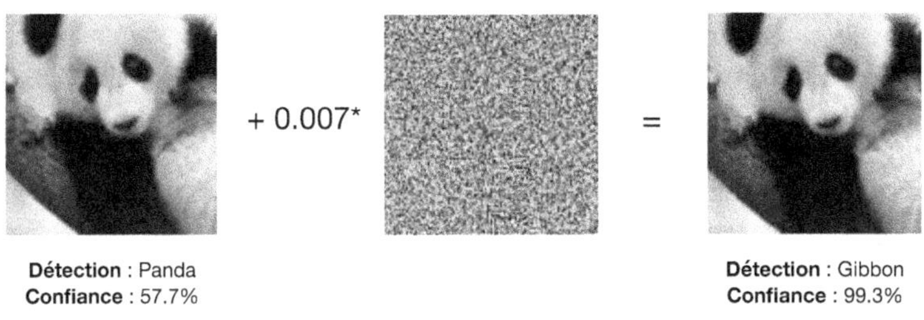

Figure 4: Illustration of the impact of noise on the recognition of an animal on an image.

In some cases, the robustness of our systems to error, minute detail and noise is lacking. As if the error, or the lack of information, silently indicated to us the importance of its role, as if a whisper in our ear could dictate a whole world to us. Artificial neural network algorithms feed on errors to adjust the weighting of the links between each neuron. These measure the difference between the outputs proposed by the algorithm and those hoped for. They perform a backpropagation of this error (backpropagation of the gradient). The learning then lies in the ability of the algorithm to adjust the synaptic weights to optimize the desired result.

Biology teaches us a lot about the meaning of information through the code of life. By observing the living, we note the process of reproduction and that of cell division. DNA is then perceived as a heritage passed down from generation to generation. On the scale of one individual, this information is multiplied from cell to cell. The DNA copy is made and the heritage is inherited. DNA carries the whole information, this essential whole which characterizes the whole. It carries thousands of genes that reflect the traits of the individual. These genes are the subject of numerous studies because they are the source of the synthesis of molecules associated with specific functions. Since the beginning of humanity, man has been able to pass on part of this heritage.

In its sense and beauty, the biological mode of operation poses surprising questions. Part of the genetic makeup of RNA is ignored by the biological process. One example among others is that of introns, portions of RNA that seem to be useless. If a part of the sequence is very useful, a cutting process is performed by the splice OSOME (Figure 5). The latter makes it possible to ignore (or even repair) certain sequences useless in the synthesis of proteins. Specialists have long wondered about the meaning of these segments which do not provide any information necessary for our biological processes. Even to the point that our system will make cuts to ignore them. This is the splicing process. Portions of non-coding RNA, they raise questions. Could this be a mistake of nature? The researchers had put forward the hypothesis of a biological vestige resulting from a virus which marked our species until it left its mark in our genetic code. Today, we may have the meaning of their existence. Far from being useless, their presence would prevent the dangerous formation of RNA-DNA hybrids, which would have the consequence of harming the stability of our genome. Genotoxic structures would thus be prevented thanks to the existence of introns. A reminder of the importance of what at first glance seems unnecessary. If the story was written in music, the introns could be perceived as an absence of information necessary to preserve silence? Can there be breaks in the middle of a masterpiece. A symbol of vital vibrato? The philosopher Pyrrhon of Elis already taught us around 360 BC. AD that ataraxia, wisdom, was not possible without aphasia, silence. Nature appreciates silence.

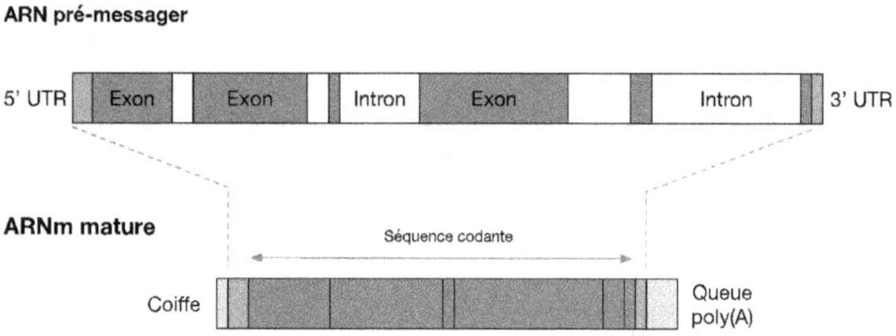

Figure 5: Illustration of the splicing process which allows the removal of introns.

Henri Atlan defended a model of the self-organization of systems thanks to disorder and noise (this is informational noise). He describes the importance of noise in reducing information redundancy and enriching the organization of a system. He clarifies his theory considering a communication channel between two subsystems of a more global system. The transmission of a message between these two sub-components can be done with or without noise. In the event that there is no noise, then the amount of information of the overall system is maintained. On the other hand, in the case where noise appears during transmission, the overall system contains more information, because there is less redundancy. This idea of using noise as an ingredient of organization at all scales: biological, sociological, but also artificial intelligence, is quite remarkable and remains relevant today. An observation which would lead Milad Doueihi to affirm that: "Forgetting and chance are the great obstacles to a true autonomy of these animated creatures (digital avatar), with limitless memory."

We have seen the importance of error in understanding the performance of algorithms, but it also exists in network science. The way men are connected to each other. The social capital defended by sociologist Ronald Burt is based on a measure of redundancy that must be reduced to optimize its position in a network. He defends the hypothesis of the cultural, intellectual and informative richness of an individual subject subjected to external stimuli of various kinds. Just like a computer specialist building algorithms, which could be considered informational noise signals related to biology or anthropology. However, genetic algorithms are bio-inspired and it is precisely this richness of complementarity of non-redundant signals that brings this type of opportunity. In this register, maximizing entropy (the physical measure of disorder) is an opportunity, and no longer a loss of information. For our online recommendation systems, our information sources are calibrated to satisfy our minds with minimal risk taking and low error rate. Here the error is offering content to a user who will not read or view it. He will not access forbidden ideas. It is, however, in an article or a work proposed by mistake, that inspiration can arise from our complex cognitive systems. A new element that suddenly enlightens our mind, forges conceptual links, and makes us grow. Perhaps our digital representations lack a way of saving chance. This chance is absent from the algorithms which systematically think for us.

We must cultivate error, the random, the spontaneous, as nature dictates. In this I have always had a great admiration for error, especially when it is committed by men. They appear all the greater in their deep weaknesses and wounds. Error in this sense is a deprivation of knowledge, as the philosopher Spinoza affirmed, as well as the mathematician René Descartes. Error, if it is the opposite of truth, is certainly a path towards the truth, an essential stage of life and the need of knowledge, far from the desires of possession. Symbols of grazes on our raw hearts, which little by little shape them and transform them into a crystal or smoke, an ultimate and indelible mark of our humanity and our elevation.

What would have become of us without the marks and the still deep imprints of our mistakes? It is by starting in the wrong directions that we usually find our way. Paths which are rich in their diversity and their learning power. There are certain categories of mistakes in life that need to be made. It is then a race for adventure as indicated by its Latin etymological origin (*error*). Some make you lose money; others make you suffer; some make you blush, and others make you laugh. All these mistakes are building blocks. Our environment is so complex that it almost imposes them on us. If it is fashionable to perceive failure as a path to success, it seems above all that making mistakes is the ultimate possibility that life offers us to make ourselves unique. Novelty can only appear through some form of error. The philosopher Gaston Bachelard reminded us that knowledge cannot do without error. We have seen it, it is even sometimes by mistake that it happens to us.

Whatever the future of our intelligent systems and the thinking machine, room for error must be cultivated. Man is unable to transcribe all decisions into the frozen and cold code of the machine. They will have to organize themselves in the image of life and of our already functional artificial neural networks. It is possible that what appear to be man's weaknesses (limited memory, chance, error) is in fact his real strength, and what appears to be the strengths of the thinking machine are in fact its main weakness. To adjust this digital nature, it will be necessary to transmit to it what sums up our essence, our philosophy, our codes and our ethics, our values, and our weaknesses. It will then be necessary to leave the machine the possibility of learning from its mistakes and our mistakes. This process will allow it to reach and accelerate its evolution.

If we have dealt with the importance of error and the apparent mathematical language of the world, there is another essential subject for understanding our reality. This prism is that of the value of the word and of the language. André Comte-Sponville connects the two, specifying that it is not the universe that is written in mathematical language, as Galileo wanted; it is the human brain which translates the silence of the universe, which is its mother tongue and mute, into mathematical language. Our languages offer reality an additional domain of abstraction. Again, at this layer of abstraction, words evolve with the digital man.

CHAPTER VII
A word to build a whole world
Where the words hide a meaning.

Life, time and language make us forget our childhood questions. The simplest questions, and certainly those which hold the promise that a curious man will be able to live amazed by all that surrounds him. These wonders are tarnished each time a word comes to settle on them to dominate what cannot be. It is more our thought encapsulated in a word, than an undeniable reality. If it is a blast on a wound, the word is painful.

Everything has a word like
It's all a word
Just like the word is an
All.

Those that impress me the most are certainly Constructivism, Doubt, Life, Death, Love, the Fantastic, Consciousness and the Eternal. The universe, space, but also water, earth, man and time, the primitive word par excellence. All these things strike me as surprising and unexpected. The sun, life, time have a much greater depth than the artifices of their simple words.

Speaking and repeating the word makes us forget its deep reality, as if we can know it otherwise. The philosopher Henri Bergson taught us that the things that language describes have been cut out from reality by human perception with a view to human work. He offers a look at the evolution of words: "They are no longer so crudely utilitarian. They remain utilitarian however." [30]

Without these words, what do we understand? Some words are doing us a disservice. They give a meaning, a shell, an existence to what is, beyond everything, more unknown than known, more incredible than believable, more uncontrollable than controllable, more sudden than chosen, more unacceptable than acceptable. Thinker Roman Osipovich Jakobson will emphasize the distinction between the word and the thing to which it refers. There will always be a distorting mirror between the word and the world, the same mirror intervenes between the physical world and the digital world.

A word has the gift of great things and great men, it is easily recognized, but so poorly understood. The word reassures, it poses and imposes itself. However, it tarnishes the possibility of constant wonder. Yes, of course, what I see is the sea. Yes, of course, it is our planet. The evidence is such to affirm that we are men and that we come to life. But what are all these complex and so elusive things? Who can claim to understand them, to understand these instances as what they intrinsically are and not in their abstraction in thought or spirit? The words that will emerge know things about us that we do not know about them, René Char taught us.

No one pretends to understand the complexity of the things and the models carried by all these words. While all men use words every day with amazing ease, no one lives up to them. This is where all the wonder and weakness of language reside, all the weakness and wonder of life. Our right to admire the world is shared and identical. We are equal in this. This thought erases in a single stroke all the bitterness that could prevent a man from crying out his despair for a society which will be (or at least appear), generation after generation for centuries and millennia, a perceived degradation of the wisdom of the people, old. Politics, success, money, thugs, crooks and egos, liars, thieves, misers, and cheaters in this sense, modestly become again words like any other. The naive man goes to bed forgetting them.

Life teaches us about the existence of dangerous words. Consciousness, artificial life, the planet, artificial intelligence, the future, come with some concerns. What future reality will arise for them? It is possible that they are supplanted by a newborn whose letters, order and meaning I do not know. They will thrill a whole world for a moment, like Blockchain, the quantum computer, *big data,* marketing, general artificial intelligence, finance, power, and influence. They will feed the discussions of the cottages and even the bank accounts of those who talk about them and practice them with the greatest skill. And then, finally, they will become unnamed banality. They will become words again, like any other. Maybe they will even disappear.

These words of artifice are not the words of poor people. Is this why those people keep their feet on the ground, full of common sense, while the words of artifice serve to explain the impossible and the incomprehensible in the drift of reason? It is by this type of *'fire-words'* that for years the domestic animal was a movable good, [32] and that, without any surprise, money continues to work. It took years to consider domestic animals as living beings endowed with sensitivity. Money always works...

Words are available to us all the time and too often even without thinking, without pronouncing them, without thinking them. They let us believe in mastery and control. Curiously, they offer themselves almost equally to the ignorant and to the genius. Would it suffice to have more to understand more? With each new word, the mirage is present. To have less would be to look at the world without artifice. It would also be asking more questions. Children's questions are simple. Yet they are hidden behind the words. Like the acceptance of a gigantic endless ignorance, man will finally have delegated his knowledge to the Word. A clever pirouette of wisdom, but it cannot be done without a certain dose of error, again, a source of an intellectual minima order.

CHAPTER VIII
A language that loses its words

Where it is about digital language.

Our most common mistakes are certainly our language mistakes. Do we have to correct them or correct the spelling? Some linguists maintain that the error having a legitimate origin, guides us towards evolution. In 1931, the linguist Henri Frei would offer us a grammar of mistakes. Faults which carry a meaning and express a need. Therefore, the error is reflected as a stealthy signal for the future. William Labov, one of the founders of modern sociolinguistics would argue that faults can be the engine of the evolution of a language. A spontaneous mutation of certain characters and a natural selection of the language are then perceptible, like living things.

If our words are imprecise, our ideas are pale and timid, and our sentences inaccurate and often imperfect. We can still hope that the baseness of our faults lifts us towards a goal: by making mistakes, we practice After all, even mistakes disappear with time. Laws and rules are evolving to make what was acceptable, acceptable and what was unacceptable, unacceptable. No language thinks: but no one thinks except with a language, except thanks to language, even if sometimes against it - which reminds us of the philosopher, André Comte-Sponville.

Another projection of this measure is the Chinese chamber thought experiment. It imagines an individual who does not speak the Chinese language in a room where he/she has access to all the rules necessary to construct sentences in Chinese. The person could then pretend, thanks to these rules, to have a mastery of the language vis-à-vis an external interlocutor, even though this individual would not understand the sentences he/she constructed. Speaking a language is obviously much more than constructing or understanding words and sentences. This experience alerts us to our artificial intelligences which, even if they know how to imitate the use of words, have no awareness, nor experience. Perceiving meaning, even through ontology, semantics or mathematical analyzes, does not correspond to awareness of meaning for our machines. This image proposed by American philosopher John Searle in the 1980s reveals the notable difference that can exist between a program that mimics intelligence on the one hand and what intelligence is. However, since Alan Turing and the famous imitation game, we no longer know how to distinguish the true from the false.

What has the power of digital technology done with our languages? For if a language loses its words, thousands of words lose their language. Thousands of inconsolable orphans. If digital technology invents/creates? a word, it is little consolation for all these sacrifices. Some languages have disappeared, others have become invisible to the cybersphere. In the digital space, languages are purified. The digital sphere can only be seen through the diving glasses of the Google search engine. It offers a spectrum of vision that is far from being panoramic. The international linguistic society estimates the number of languages at nearly 7,000. This richness reflects our diversity. Of these, more than 2,000 are already threatened. The impact of digital technology is unforgivable. Of the 10 million most visible pages, the vast majority are exclusively in English (over 75 %). Only 5 % of languages are likely to be accessible, and most would not even be represented. English crushes any other language in this 2.0 society, which needs to be simple to be visible, simple to go fast. The image has gradually replaced the word. More suitable and more adapted to an evanescent digital society, which thinks quickly. The quest for influence leaves too little chance for words. The information overload of our billions of web pages is certainly one of the causes. A difficult choice must be made between maintaining our differences on the one hand and opportunistic mimicry on the other. This mimicry that pushes us to envy what the other has. In this sense, men like more what they imagine that others possess. A thirst that forces our algorithms to erase differences and grows our crops to resemble one another? (Spinoza's Doctrine of the Imitation of Affects), to fade to the point that some anthropologists are asking if their science has any interest for our epoch. Let us reassure ourselves and take a closer look at the new linguistic creations of our digital society. *Leet, emoticon* and *smiley* are our new ways of thinking.

CHAPTER IX
A language that wins words
Of our new words and our new languages.

We gain new words and even new languages. These words have been created over the years and in writings to characterize the transformation expected and experienced by our species. This change is particularly noticeable in the field of science fiction and futurology. From poets and great scientists who have set unpublished terms in the language of their times. These are still relevant today and represent a picture of the new perspectives of man. Let us note for example in the writings of Dante, Teilhard de Chardin, Herbert Marshall McLuhan or Vernor Vinge the terms of transhumanization (spiritual transformation, sublimation of love to the point of reaching paradise), of the Omega point (final point of unification of the universe), noogenesis (the emergence of the human spirit), a global village (idea that new technologies are changing the world into a global village) and technological singularity (forecast of a meteoric increase in knowledge and technologies). These are the signs of a foreseen evolution of our flesh, our cultures and our minds captured in writing. In particular, the singularity could mark the decline of the differences between physical and virtual reality and between man and machine.

More anecdotally (but significantly), the arrival in the French language of the terms geek, buzz (2010), then tweet (2012), and hashtag (2015) will not succeed in compensating for the loss of historical terms that have aged badly. Mâtineau, myrtiforme or futurition have made their final bows. Let's welcome our pirate languages, *Leet* or *emoticon* glyphs and other *smileys*. We advocate the diversity of languages. So, it will come as no surprise to welcome the *Leet* language on some social networks. A desire to seduce *Geek* users, to keep them within closer reach of the keyboard. Is this good news for the diversity of languages or more precisely *357-c3 un3 80nn3 n0uv3113 p0u2 14 d1v325173 d35 14n9u3?* How often have we had the disagreeable experience of finding our humanity disguised behind an incomprehensible list of letters and numbers, whatever their meaning or objective What should our words say when they are deprived of some of their letters to inject numbers that have only visual meaning? The SMS language, although purely digital, has caused much ink to flow. Some did not understand it, others found it simpler, faster: a side effect relating to the limited number of words that could be transmitted by SMS with older generations of mobile phones. Our shortened words have found a way of living. They appeal to those who *Who Are In Search of Lost Time.*

We can then ask ourselves how far it is possible to simplify a language. In the extreme, when all elegance is gone, what will remain? Eventually, certainly, a great silence as at the beginning, but before that, writing without words and a few symbols? Like a throwback to our past: a simplified pictogram to restore a purity worthy of an unattached signal. Crumbly digital emotions that don't even deserve a word, not a sentence. This is how a new generation of glyphs saw their opportunity. The famous emoticons (e.g., , ,). Simplified images of faces with varied emotions which are so practical to convey feelings. These would be more suitable and stronger than the simple, aging words of our language. In any case, it is certain that these latter do not offer the same experience to the digital generation. A success so rich, that the brand with the apple made it a selling point of its last phone at the forefront of technology. Perhaps one day we will be nostalgic for a time when letters carried well-posed and chosen words.

Today, our lexemes are reduced to the order of pictograms. To understand how far we are going, the author who still wants to use words on his smartphone can automatically convert them into more effective images, the removal of sensitive words by images, like a service rendered. An illustration of a digital world driven by images, by appearances. Artifices that we seize through our screens. Tricks to the detriment of meaning.

The philosopher Michel Serres referred to the emergence of information and communication technologies as the third major anthropological revolution. After all, the *Leet* language, *emoticons,* our words won and lost are perhaps the signal reflecting our cultural changes. A reflection of our journey from a traditional to a digital era. A signal of low amplitude, but which reveals what could become of i digital man. The work of Vladimir Abikh (Figure 6) represents some of our emoticons on a surprising medium: sandstone. The artist explains, "Sandstone has provided us with data on ancient civilizations across millennia and will present people in the future with the super-fast, virtual history of our time."

Figure 6: A new generation of glyphs has emerged. A work by artist Vladimir Abikh depicting evolution.

Losing words, does it reduce our field of vision of this abstraction of reality? Gaining other words, does it open a new spectrum on this reality? The double meaning illustrates the double life that is taking shape. Friendship, love, trust, space, intelligence, memory, influence, identity are terms that have a new meaning for this new image. New lexemes which indicate that our picture of reality is moving with technology. They write a new form of reality in new words.

CHAPTER X
A strange power emerges from language
Where words form much more than sentences.

Anthropologists have widely found that a language carries the memory of time. Language is a symbol of what the simplest can create and transform into complex articulations. Simple phonemes to a limited number. Our species articulates words that carry meaning and allow communication. A miracle as strong as that carried by music whose constituents are only modest notes. Notes whose subtle and organized layouts can offer you unparalleled depth of emotion. We cannot reasonably compile an exhaustive list of works that offer this form of miracle. I felt it for the first time thanks to the work of Franz Schubert - Piano Trio in E flat, op. 100. These are the leaders: works that illustrate the richness that can be built on the basis of elements which, after all, seem elementary when separated. A miracle sought after by all artists, but which holds a secret that seems inexplicable and cannot be automated. A reflection of the reasons that can push scientists to imagine consciousness emerging from fairly simple bricks. A consciousness that could be perceived as a double integration of information and signals. A property that emerges on the scale of the whole, and that cannot be explained simply on smaller scales. An emerging property at the scale of the whole. In this image, some sentences symbolize so much more than their mere words. This power is wonderfully illustrated in the first lines of the poet Louis Aragon, "Que serais-je sans toi", in *the unfinished novel* published in 1956. You will find much more than these words:

> "What would I be without you who came to meet me
> What would I be without you a sleeping heart
> That this hour stopped on the face of the watch
> What would I be without you this stammering"

In addition to carrying emotions, language has this last power, that of carrying history and knowledge, that of telling the history of men. We can affirm that the history of men is written with the history of languages and vice versa. The phylogeny of Austronesian languages studying the links between related languages reveals the pioneering journey of ancient sailors from the soil of Madagascar to Easter Island.

Writing is also a major development, as Stephen Hawking reminds us. Its birth meant that "information could be passed from generation to generation other than genetically through DNA." The first passage of man as a creator of a reusable resource and synonymous with progress, knowledge, and a science that should no longer be erased.

We have gradually extricated ourselves from our constraints of space and time. Technologies extend these ambitions and possibilities. Man then wants to preserve what he has created and exceed the limits to offer himself a chance. A chance to save him, chance to save his self. Knowledge must now reach extraordinary temporal distances and spatial durations. The conservation of this heritage is a key issue in an era of doubt and transformation.

CHAPTER XI
Return beyond time and space
Bringing our knowledge as far as possible, in time and space.

Everything that comes out of our time and space scale belongs to a form of beyond: beyond everyone, beyond us, to eternity. Borders intrigue us, disturb us, offer us a framework, and push us towards philosophy. The question of what is important is as relative as it is universal. What assessment can we make of humanity, of its knowledge, of its learning? It would be impossible to choose by reason anything in the immensity of our works. What can we do if our history has made choices by collective memory, by writings, by feelings, of what to keep from us, what to transmit? A dilemma, which even if one is obliged to give an answer, nevertheless brings an attempt at clarification.

A first response was brought in 1977 by the surprising ambition of Voyager records. The latter enclose sounds and images of the Earth on gilded copper discs covered with aluminum. Having left to explore space, the planets, they take their place on the edge of the Voyager probes. The Voyager 1 probe is now in interstellar space. Along the way, it will have contributed to the observation of the rings of Jupiter, to the discovery of new moons of Jupiter and Saturn. We owe it a lot, and yet the on-board computer is ridiculously underpowered compared to the latest trendy phone in our pocket. We owe him the magnificent work of Carl Sagan, a pale blue dot. The title of this work is inspired by the unique photo which at the time was the most distant observation of our Earth (Figure 7). It was taken at a distance of 6.4 billion kilometers from the latter.

Figure 4 : Photograph known as "A pale blue dot" representing the Earth and obtained from space by Voyager 1 on February 14, 1990.

In 1994, the American astronomer would say a lot about this look back from so far away [39] : "Look at this little point again. It's here. It is our home. It's us. On it is everyone you love, everyone you know, everyone you have heard of, all human beings who have never lived. All the sum of our joys and our sufferings, thousands of religions with assured convictions, ideologies and economic doctrines, all hunters and gatherers, all heroes and all cowards, all creators and destroyers of civilizations, all kings and all peasants, all young loving couples, all fathers and mothers, all hopeful children, inventors and explorers, all moral teachers, all corrupt politicians, all superstars, all the supreme guides, all the saints and sinners in the history of our species have lived here, on this speck of dust hanging in a ray of sunshine."

Today, the probe is even further away from us. It transformed Sagan's still respectful and optimistic view of who we are into something more invisible and modest. Ultimately, it is the most accurate picture we can have of who we are, so small compared to the infinite Universe, yet so huge on the quantum scale. The Voyager probe, its distance, its journey, offers us a neutral perspective. From there, the truth is seen, and the correctness adjusts. At the end of its path, nothing will remain visible of this Earth, of our Earth. We will no longer guess anything of what exists, of what lives and which is all too often worried. Then, there, finally, perhaps, we will be able to understand what we were from the beginning. A grain of nothing in a gigantic space, a miraculous chance of nothingness. A species with unimaginable creative power to the point of affording us this unthinkable cliché. A species that might one day deserve to be known by another life form. A species that can make us proud and humble. This probe has reduced and sublimated us to what we are. Men who are equal in that they are nothing but carry everything.

Traveling, Voyager 1 should one day meet the fate of another star. 40,000 years from now. Voyager 1 now sails more than 22 billion kilometers from Earth. This probe is the most distant human object. God only knows what will be left of us when it reaches this star. In the end, maybe, yes, it's this record that will survive us. If so, to what have we reduced what we are? What we know? What have we done with it?

Science answers this mystery: that of safeguarding our heritage. This heritage is both the code and the message sent to the universe; a message whose ambition is to summarize what constitutes the wealth of our Earth. This ark of knowledge must make it possible to survive and to give meaning to our species beyond the confines of our galaxy. Our technologies allow us to dream of knowledge that goes beyond our humanity. Knowledge that is not simply lost in the careless hands of a fragile man who would risk dropping it.

CHAPTER XII
Humanity from images to words
The message carried by a bottle in the cosmic sea.

The message sent as a bottle in the interstellar sea was signed by the 39th president of the United States Jimmy Carter in 1977. The words are offered to another civilization: "This is a gift of a small distant world, a pledge of our sounds, our science, our images, our music, our thoughts and our feelings. We try to survive our time so that we can live in yours. We hope that one day, after solving the problems we face, we will join a community of galactic civilizations. This recording represents our hope and determination, and our goodwill in a vast and awe-inspiring universe."

To understand the meaning of this attempt, we must remember that we are desperately looking for traces of life on other planets. However, we cannot imagine ourselves alone, we do not want to accept it and for good reason, mathematics forbids us to do so, through the famous Drake equation. The latter makes it possible to estimate the number of extraterrestrial civilizations existing in our galaxy and with which we could one day come into contact. Under a strong scenario, the equation would lead to over 36 extraterrestrial civilizations in our Milky Way. A figure to be taken with extreme caution.

It is indeed to the unknown that we address our work. In addition to a soundtrack, 116 images were selected, in order to make our humanity speak in a few snapshots. A task led by a dedicated committee under the leadership of Carl Sagan. Among the most important secrets contained in this record, it is obviously that of life. Finally, what understand life to be. In the order of the images, we perceive the story that wishes to be recounted to these extraterrestrials, the very essence of what makes us. The first images are mathematical, like a reflection of this universal representation of our world and which will have the merit of freezing things to a minimum. They give a time reference and size that ser? is present on almost all other images.

It all starts with the representation of the atoms essential to life: hydrogen, carbon, oxygen, nitrogen, sulfur, and phosphorus. We see them as the prime components made up of a nucleus and a varying number of electrons. These components are necessary for life, in fact they alone make up almost all forms of life. The human body, for example, is made up of oxygen, carbon and hydrogen. They represent respectively 65 %, 18.5 % and 9.5 % of the total body weight.

Then, their combined arrangements are shown. The molecule and the macromolecules, the bases (nucleics) of life: thymine, adenine, cytosine and guanine. Clever assemblages of these atoms the nature of whose appearance on Earth still keeps secrets.

In the following images, we understand that some bases can be held together, thanks to hydrogen bonds. This is how adenine binds to thymine and guanine to cytosine. An essential complementarity which allows life to be duplicated and information to be transmitted. The double helix follows: DNA. This extraordinary molecule has a design that is as elegant as it is important to carry life. Strata of base pairs stack up and cling to each other. We then traverse the images of cell division that appear along the DNA replication. They give a first meaning to life. They reveal part of its secret, a propeller that doubles up the better to endure and reproduce what itself. And then, the image of a human appears: thanks to Erwin Chargaff, Rosalind Franklin, Oswald Theodore Avery, James Dewey Watson, Francis Crick. Years of research and discoveries gathered and summarized in a few meaningful images.

Our anatomy is then detailed, followed by the cells, the fetus, the birth, the family, love and so many simple images, but the essentials.

Universal, often banal, and classic things in our lives. Things which are, however, unique, and rare when we think of them outside our planet, outside our existence. There must be something elsewhere and it is to this elsewhere that we send the image of the Earth. People, geography, botany, animals, culture, sport, agriculture, architecture, medicine, scenes from everyday life, the sun and music.

From these fields were chosen a few men and a few works from among the billions possible. Beethoven, the Sydney Opera House, Andromeda, the Sun,

Jupiter, Saturn, the Earth, man and strangers from all cultures. These contain a semblance of eternity. A sequoia, a dolphin, a dancer from Bali, a house, the Great Wall of China, the Taj Mahal, the X-ray, the microscope, the Golden Gate, a computer, a car, a city. Already there's a form of dizziness. A book, or, more exactly, a page of the foundational classic *System of the world* by Isaac Newton. If you haven't read it, hurry up. Aliens might do it before you! A cosmonaut, a rocket, a sunset, the music. All these things have a fair and precise meaning in our lives. Unique things in the eyes of our artists and observers of the beyond. These things which, as we know today, have little chance of surviving like their creators. Their representations will undoubtedly survive us. Maybe that will be enough to give them new life, a form of eternity by surpassing humanity.

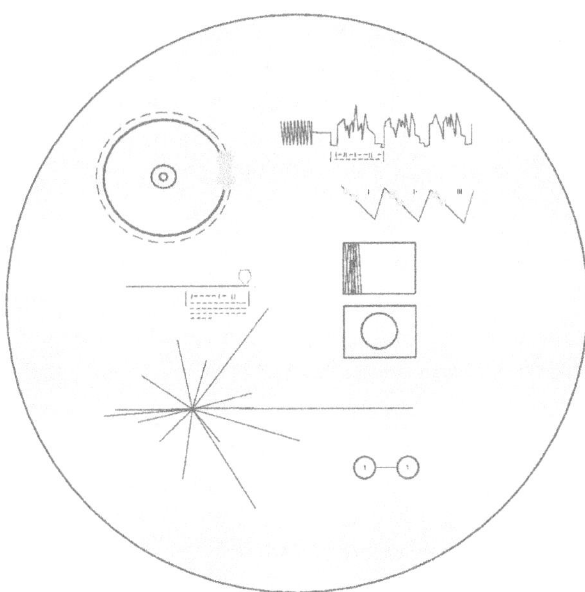

Figure 8: Image of the traveling disc. It contains valuable instructions necessary for its reading.

From so far away, the disc looks at us, but no longer sees us. On the other side, we look at the sky, towards the disc, but we no longer perceive it. It seems so far away, as if out of time.

Do these existential things exist?

Now they seem timeless
Out of our time
From that far it doesn't seem to make sense anymore
We believe it has disappeared for a moment in the silence
In space
And then…
We turn the record
Time reappears

It forces is everywhere, even far away, in the middle of nothing. It has the better of us, because to read this record you need a measure of time. We perceive the instructions for reading it on its face (Figure 8). This reading time which allows it to be understood. To study the details, it is necessary to refer to the official description of the NASA. In fact, in the upper left corner of the disc is a drawing of a phonograph and the stylus that accompanies it. Around this illustration in binary arithmetic is the correct speed for the rotation of the recording. Time therefore appears but must be specified. The rotation lasts 3.6 seconds. To ensure understanding, this period is expressed in units of 0.70 billionth of a second, which is the period associated with a fundamental transition of the hydrogen atom.

To reflect a little more the importance of this time on this face of the disc, let us observe its electroplating. This goldsmith's technique which is used for the reproduction of objects using a mold connected to the negative pole of a battery and which is then covered with a layer of metal. The electroplating on the record sleeve is an ultra-pure source of uranium-238 with a radioactivity of approximately 0.00026 microcurie. The regular decay of this source of uranium in daughter isotopes makes it a radioactive clock. Half of uranium-238 is expected to decay in more than 4.5 billion years. Extraterrestrial receivers could then, by examining this two-centimeter diameter area, calculate the time elapsed since the uranium was placed. To do this, they would simply have to measure the quantity of daughter elements of the remaining uranium 238. Still, a matter of time. As if the secret of all understanding finally came from that. A sublime message offered to us by imagining and creating this record. Time is indeed at the origin of everything. Knowledge and life rest and bathe in this time. Outside, they no longer have any meaning.

CHAPTER XIII
An ark of knowledge
When knowledge and life crash into our moon.

The first traces of the *homo* genus date back 2.5 million years. We are in a way the vestiges of this history. What have we inherited from others? The Egyptians succeeded, in an almost obsessive quest for eternity, in passing on some of the 3000 years history of their civilization. This feat was made possible through objects, hieroglyphic writings engraved on the walls or placed on papyri (for example the book of the dead), but also architectural gems whose construction still retains mysteries. I hope that these works will travel a few more millennia. They know how to hide their secrets from men, the better to preserve themselves. In comparison, our modern and digital people sometimes seem like modest contributors to virtual empires, which are erased with a click.

Protecting knowledge and ensuring the persistence of our knowledge is a task fraught with symbolism and importance. Especially when we hope to make it outlive time and overcome space. Nova Spivack is the co-founder of *The Ark Mission Foundation*. His mission is simple: to ensure the preservation of human knowledge, to ensure it in the face of the growing risk that *homo sapiens* carries on itself and on the planet. Preservation imagined, at best, and further in time. The solutions considered are numerous and are not limited to a storage place on Earth. For preservation, other stars in the solar system are being considered. The Moon is one of them. The American entrepreneur confides: "Our work is the material safeguard of this planet. Our role is to make sure that we protect our heritage. Both our knowledge and our biology. We kind of have to plan for the worst."

To ensure this mission, in the tradition of the Voyager disc, a team worked on the development of 25 nickel discs. These can withstand more than a thousand degrees, and do not deteriorate in contact with cosmic rays. Therefore, they seem ready for the passage of time. They remain readable after more than 14 billion years. A differential that makes one wonder what our words are used for, which are so easily erased when they are placed on a piece of paper or a digital corner. All our other works suddenly seem evanescent and so fragile. Perhaps this is ultimately what gives them a meaning, a sensitivity?

More than a stone, symbol of the ruin of the past, more than debris, symbol of collapse, they are more than a noise coming out of silence. They are what will be left of us when there is nothing left. As if touching would instantly turn us to ashes. To get an idea of this passage of time, remember that the Earth is 4.543 billion years old and that it will cease to be habitable within 1.75 to 3.25 billion years. Let's not talk about our passage, your passage and mine. They are not even worth a click of the fingers.

A version of this nickel Ark was embarked on the SpaceIL Beresheet space probe in 2019. Beresheet, whose symbolic name corresponds to the first word of the bible meaning "in the beginning ". It is profoundly meaningful and is associated with the terms bara (he created), berit (the covenant), and shit (the foundation). This probe was placed in orbit on February 22, 2019 by SpaceX's Falcon 9 rocket. One of many companies founded and run by successful entrepreneur Elon Musk. On April 4, 2019 the probe was this time placed in lunar orbit.

The Ark has 30 million Wikipedia pages, but also other forms of knowledge and information. Perhaps this is our major contribution of this century, a collaborative online encyclopedia which is more comprehensive than ever before. A digital work to replace the others: temples, the great Wall, cathedrals, pyramids, cave paintings. Our last work has a considerable advantage, it is a mobile work, light, which can be replicated effortlessly. Some common attributes with life that, maybe, will allow it to survive?

The disc contained the bricks of life. Human DNA samples were added at the last moment as well as a set of very special little beings: Tardigrades or water bears (Figure 9). At just over a millimeter, these slow walkers are very resilient eukaryotes. They can survive in extreme conditions thanks to their talent for cryptobiosis. Completely freezing their state in the absence of water, this extremophile regenerates under favorable conditions. In the laboratory, they have been observed for up to nine years in a state of cryptobiosis. Strong enough to live in the Himalayas and even survive in deep ice. We don't really know any limits for them. It is perhaps even their presence that will allow the record to resist.

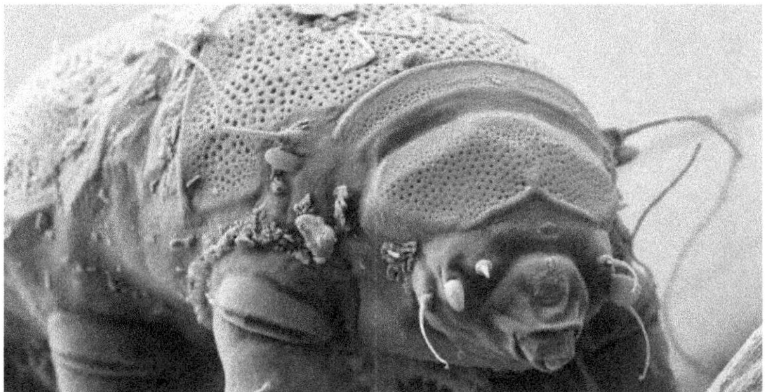
Figure 5 : The tardigrade is an extremophilic species.

It was in the last days before launch that the decision to integrate them into the disc was taken. More precisely, between the 25 discs, resin encapsulates the little beings. A few thousand tardigrades are imprisoned, but ultimately this has the effect of making the nickel strata more robust. A detail that is important, because in its attempt to land on the moon, the Israeli private explorer would end up crashing on lunar soil on April 11, 2019. The mission is a failure, it is destroyed, but the ark may have survived, and the last-minute addition helped to consolidate the disks. Scientists are confident about the chances of an intact lunar library.

This project reveals man's desire to offer his knowledge a quest for immortality. Are we addressing this knowing to ourselves or to an alien life form? If it is the second hypothesis, caution would be required.

In 2015, Yuri Milner and Stephen Hawking encouraged the search for extraterrestrial life forms through the *Breakthrough Initiatives* program. In particular the *Breakthrough Message* and *Listening programs* aiming to listen to the messages coming from space and to transmit our own. The goal is to build messages that could be read by an advanced civilization. We are warned, however, about the risk of responding to a possible message: "We must be careful not to respond until we have developed our technology a little further. Meeting a more advanced civilization, at our current stage, might be a bit like the first inhabitants of America meeting Christopher Columbus."

To go further, it would be necessary to make something even smaller than a disk, lighter. Once again, life provides us with a solution.

CHAPTER XIV
Data will survive us
Where we want to perpetuate knowledge differently.

If we can't live forever, can we make this dream come true to for our data? After all, we may be, as some think, information and nothing else. If digital information preservation solutions exist and are widely used, what can we pass on to our descendants? A USB key, a hard drive, an RFID chip, a magnetic strip, a cloud access code, a social network account or more surprisingly and yet very natural, a few grams of DNA. This option is not utopian and the idea of exploiting, of programming organic matter to store information is at the very basis of life and its meaning, as well as many technological innovations. This approach has been validated experimentally by encoding the digital data (a computer file) with the four nucleic bases (Figure 10). DNA synthesis corresponds to writing data, and sequencing to reading. While the cost of the synthesis procedure is still very high, the benefits are also significant. A few grams of DNA would be capable of storing an exabyte (10^{18} bytes) of data. In this way, all the data ever collected digitally would only occupy a few square meters.

As a further benefit, the data would be kept intact for hundreds, thousands, or even more than a million years. The maximum shelf life of DNA is estimated at 1.5 million years under ideal temperature conditions. These timescales represent a dream of eternity for a computer and an eternally young and volatile man.

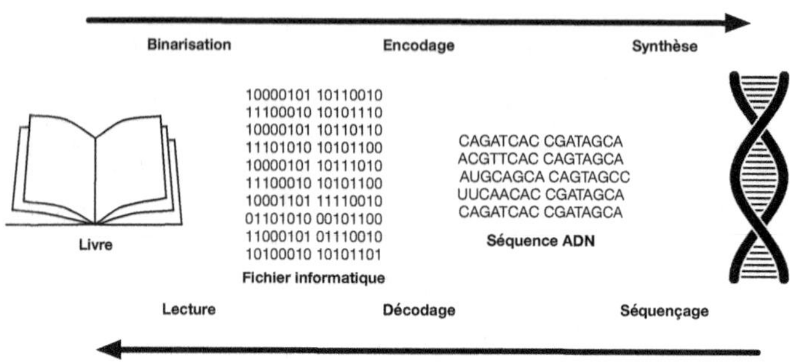

Figure 10: Process of writing and reading digital content on an organic medium: DNA.

George Church's book *Regenesis* was synthesized into DNA, then sequenced to recover its entirety. The approach has been proven in many cases, including in living bacteria. The idea of providing each work with a DNA strand, was abandoned for ethical reasons.

In 2017, a small black and white film was encoded as DNA in living cells and then successfully played again. The diameter of the macromolecule is just over two nanometers, and the pairs are only separated by 0.33 nanometers. This film is therefore the smallest in history.

Neuroscientist Seth Shipman used the following formula to qualify our ambitions in genetic engineering: "We want to turn cells into historians." This statement is now truer than ever. However, that may be the role they had from the start.

A convergence can be observed between the two modes of transmission of information ever used by man in his great history: genetic material on the one hand, the only way to transmit on a very large time scale; and knowledge by writing, a modern approach to transmission in another format. Of the two works, however, that of nature still seems the more immutable and optimal.

CHAPTER XV
From Alexandria to a postage stamp
Where we reduce our knowledge to a postage stamp.

Access to and digitization of knowledge is an exceptional source of wealth. A manuscript from another century or several millennia will find its place on the web just like the news of a day that has just ended. One, whose importance, memory, and effort of conservation rests on millions of men, an indisputable work and respected by all; the other hardly worth an effort of reading.

> Each day is filled with information
> whose meaning disappears on a daily basis.
> This news is renewed so quickly to the point of being aged,
> hardly spoken.

Some find their place in our museums, our libraries, others in our picture boxes. Everything is there, and even more than anything.

You have to go back in time to understand the effort required to constitute a space of knowledge. The Library of Alexandria is one of the missing gems of our planet. It had the sublime ambition of bringing together in one place all the works of Greek civilization of the time. A Wonder conceived by Ptolemy I Soter, in the IIIrd century BC, and whose mission was entrusted to Demetrius Faliro, a disciple of Aristotle. The latter gathered in its golden age up to more than 700,000 volumes. A titanic work (Τιτάν) to collect and organize texts and manuscripts. Far from our information society, society wanted to gain access, above all and above all, to knowledge. This library had something in common with our digital encyclopedias, it made access to information by pooling and by grouping it in dedicated locations. Today, the web offers itself the same luxury, it pools information, almost all information. On the other hand, it has become ubiquitous, produced and accessible from any location on the planet. Our information is, however, not only from scholars. It is the product of each of us, at every moment. Accordingly, we have embarked on a path that leads us to an information overload.

Staying informed is not synonymous with knowledge or wisdom.
A knowledge society is not just an informed society.
An informed society is not a learned society.

At one time, the preciousness of information was due to its scarcity. This is what is shocking, in view of the millions of books published each year, to the point where we have seen the appearance of new machines and software. To the same extent that uncertain and unfaithful information, produced by everyone and at every moment can be taken as truth.

I like to think of the times when knowledge was a quest and to consult a manuscript a conquest. Respect for writing was associated with preciousness, going in search of a manuscript in the hope of finding it, making efforts to grant knowledge its learning a nobility formed by memory. It was not a question of making into fun a resource that had become too commonplace to merit the interest of learners. Let's be optimistic, if our digital libraries disappear, it won't be in a fire.

We now have access to new media and new formats. Since the invention of writing about 5000 years ago, man has not ceased to use all forms of support for his ideas, his drawings, his symbols, his glyphs, his syllables, his words and his stories, his beliefs, and his fears. They have been written on cave walls, stone, wet earth, papyrus, wood, semiconductors, DNA and atoms. He never stopped wanting to keep track of his works, his images, his writings. It is his work at once fictitious, mythical, realistic and scientific to which we owe all our masterpieces. The Bible, encyclopedias, our thousands of classics from Livy to Chateaubriand will have made man and his memory progress in a certain way. One of the longest, laudable and permanent tasks of this human endeavor is hidden in the books. These books, precisely all those ever created, will soon stand - very small - on a postage stamp-sized stand. All the history, made up of our stories that once filled vast monuments as grandiose as they are loaded: every single one, from the Rosetta Stone to the latest American *bestseller*, can all now find place in a space no larger than a stamp. How is this possible? Scientists have made a digital memory at the atomic scale. Here are the details. It is currently only robust up to 1 kilobyte. The researchers used an array of individual surface vacancies in a chlorine-terminated Cu (100) surface. Thanks to this process, as close as possible to the smallest of what we know how to make work, this memory would reduce, not to dust, but to atoms, all the writings in the world. From this angle, I cannot imagine or calculate the volume of information that we can put in the universe, or more simply, the volume of information that the universe contains. With such a scale of storage, one day perhaps, everyone will have this knowledge, no longer in libraries, nor on digital, but directly in an augmented head.

If the universe, from its cosmic angle, seemed unimaginable. From its atomic angle, it is immensely unthinkable. We have 10^{14} atoms in a human cell and between 10,000 and 100,000 billion cells in a human. There are no less than 10^{50} atoms on Earth, and there is no room here to write its number in the universe. In a metaphor of man as information, Stephen Hawking offers a comparison of the volume of information in our books and in our genetic makeup: "The total amount of useful information in our genes is probably one hundred million bits. [...] On the other hand, a paperback novel could contain two million bits of information. Consequently, a human is equivalent to about fifty Harry Potter books [...] The amount of information transmitted in books or via the internet is 100,000 times greater than in DNA." [50]

A grain of sand in the desert or a drop of water in the ocean could soon be the proud home of our manuscripts and books. Important as they are, soon they will be laid out on atoms are invisible to the human eye. It seems to me that everyone remains calmly in their place, at their scale and at their level of importance. The drop of water has yet this reassurance as noted by the poet and philosopher Khalil Gibran: "It contains the secrets of all the oceans." [51] Then perhaps a single atom contains the secret of the whole universe, of a man, or of two humans, male and female: the secret of humanity?

If our technology sometimes gives the impression of almost complete power and mastery of things, let us not forget our eternal ignorance.

CHAPTER XVI
What we don't know
When what we know makes us forget our ignorance.

The most important questions always seem to remain unanswered. Every step that pushes the unknown away leads us to a new unknown. The more we have seen in the heart of matter, the more mysteries we have discovered.

Top ocean scientists will tell you they know so little about the ocean. The biologist will tell you that life is a complex work and not fully understood, far from being mastered. Our planet hides mysteries for all the scientists of the world. All have one thing in common, they are humble about their years of wisdom and knowledge, having finally understood that the latter was and would remain eternally partial. It represents almost nothing with regard to the object that it has nevertheless ceaselessly and constantly sought to study. Neither a biologist nor a physicist or a novelist will be of supreme help.

From Leucippus and Democritus to Erwin Schrödinger, via Dalton, Aristotle, Michael Faraday and Ernest Rutherford, scientists have always wanted to know more about what surrounds us and turns with us in this great merry-go-round. The physicist Werner Karl Heisenberg will force us to stop to look at the uncertainty at the heart of matter. When you approach smallness, the particle, you have to admit to a part of doubt. Momentum and position are associated in the same indeterminacy. Try to determine the position of a particle, and its movement seems to partially escape you. Try to catch the movement, and its position seems to partially overtake you. It is not a question of material; we have to accept the uncertainty: the principle of uncertainty of Heisenberg.

Another image is that of entropy. This measurement of thermodynamic order forces us to accept disorder. This disorder is therefore our new order. We cannot reduce the entropy of an isolated system; it only keeps increasing. This is the second principle of thermodynamics. Physicist Roger

Penrose will make it a more universal reality. The world is becoming more complex every moment. As time advances, entropy advances. Have we entered the century of complexity? Complexity which, by increasing, seems to highlight in an even more salient way our sublime ignorance.

The quantum makes us dream; the universe makes us dream. What we discover along the way is so beautiful that we stop and struggle with our questions. What do we we really know about who we are? How can two particles know whether to attract or repel each other? If our accumulated knowledge offers us solid and gigantic libraries of things to learn, and if these things are constantly better understood, better mastered and serious, we master very little. Our successes are modest. Our feat of gaining a few years of life, our feat of flying a little higher, of thinking big enough, all these discoveries do not ultimately tell us where we come from and where we are going.

We know that the universe is made up mostly of dark matter and energy. This concerns more than 95 % of what surrounds us, it is not a minor detail. Their very natures are unknown to us, and their existence remains hypothetical. We belong to the remaining 5% that makes up the rest: the planets, the stars, our planet, living beings. We don't know much more about these substances. We have to simply accept the uncertainty: from the infinitely small to the infinitely large.

Like the landmark discoveries of Albert Einstein, which many scientists admit that without such a genius, some discoveries might not yet have been made, anything goes. Lights (?) up all at once?

In the quest for the intelligent universe, some physicists think that everything is related (for example to information). Is the answer close? Will we one day be able to predict the behavior of each man by the deterministic laws of physics? The quest is uncertain, but hoping for a law that encompasses everything, it will necessarily include us in its path. It will encompass our unconscious, our conscious, our actions, matter, antimatter, the visible, the invisible, life and death. Stephen Hawking spoke of it this way: "A complete, coherent and unified theory would be only the first step: our goal is a complete understanding of the events around us and of our own existence."

We know that within 10,000 years, the red supergiant Antares should explode into a supernova. We know that 600 million years from now, no total solar eclipse will be visible from Earth due to tidal forces. We know that stars will cease to be born in a little over a billion years. In the midst of our conversation, even as I write, I sometimes do not know which word will succeed the next. There is a paradox of scales, of the known and the unknown. Even here, Claude Shannon's information theory could attempt to predict the succession of my letters and my words.

We have never put so many minds to work on the same path to understand the issue, to discover the rules of the game. It is certain that our knowledge is accelerating. What will it reveal and when? Will we come to a wall like Max Planck's? On an event horizon? Despite having published a book entitled "nearly nothing about everything", Jean d'Ormesson will not have finally been able to provide the answers expected by his very dear Marie. We read on the back cover of the work *"One day I will go away without having said everything,"*. The words which follow, beautiful, honest and realistic about the ignorance which lulls us all, even after having made the most sublime literary promenade of the things: "What I wanted to know, I still do not know it. What will happen to us, and to you and to me, in just a few years, or maybe even tomorrow, when the time is up for our passage on this Earth, is still as obscure to me. I've heard you say many times that you want to write books that change people's lives. You haven't changed much in the transient and so terribly threatened fragility of my love for you."
Existence precedes essence, or does it succeed it? Ignorance precedes existence, or does it succeed it? Caught up in a technological leap, we forget our fragility, but also everything we are ignorant of. However, all the sciences show us to what extent a vast space and a gigantic time of discovery are always in front of us. This position of ignorance is offered even to the wisest. It humbly urges us to continue our quest. In this world of ignorant knowledge, what is the place of technology and what is the place of the digital? What images of each other and of the digital world can we carry in the midst of our space of knowledge and abstraction?

CHAPTER XVII
How to place the digital in these images of knowledge?
Where worlds complement and blend.

We have seen that our knowledge is a reflection, if not our ignorance, of our interpretation of reality with and through our artefacts and technologies. A formal encoding of a reality that can only be dealt with through actions, equations, numbers and words. It is this abstraction that has allowed us to stand out from other species through conscious thought and intelligence. Thus, the allegory of Plato's cave is universal. If we are ignorant about almost everything, we also have the power to imagine almost anything and to conceive of what in itself is beyond us. These interactions between a tangible physical world governed by empirical laws, and our representations have occupied the lives of men from the beginning of their existence (for example in primitive art). Myths, sciences, knowledge have progressed through this game of doubles, this double I. While we have very little control over these exchanges and passages from one world to another, a New World has appeared in recent years: the digital

What place can we then conceive for what seems to be a new world? Is it just a technology, or a separate reality? It is apart, but permanently exchanging with our form of reality. Even to the point that identical concepts are understood differently depending on the space. We have noted friendship, influence, reputation, information, memory, reality, which even become virtual or augmented.

Developer Tim Bray defended a vision of humans directly linked to technologies to the point that we are no longer quite the same. Considering men as ordinary users would be an obsolete vision that forgets the changing technology of man. It is therefore useful to put forward a concept closer to a digital human to illustrate this state of affairs. There might be a new digital nature to come.

The term, as indicated by many key figures in the French digital landscape, would imply a passage from one physical state to a more virtual one. It would imply the existence of a new world, that of the digital. The latter being an additional level of abstraction. This space could appear as a simple mirror almost identical or even belonging to, enhancing existing models. The fact remains that it both complicates our representations and enriches our possibilities. In this way, it provides computer scientists with languages, even an object-oriented language where programmers manipulate objects by name and make them perform tasks. A realistic abstraction from our physical world to the point that our information systems would have no other objectives than to support companies in their missions, which are well anchored in reality. They mix sociological and technical dimensions and have an impact on the physical world that they model and represent through the same important resource: information.

It is topical to think that our digital world could lead us to unprecedented power over the real world. They would share the same essence. It would then allow man to imagine modifying the realm of reality in its essence. If a new form of life emerges, whether resuscitated by genetic engineering or whether purely artificial, can it be denied a physical reality? Information could unite the three faces of perception or shed light on the unique existence of reality. Some physicists are convinced that information is the resource, the reality and at the same time the very metaphor of all reality, while mathematics is its outline.

At the frontiers of knowledge, and thanks to this additional spectrum, are added new images that artists make of our world. We can dream our art and make people dream through our art. The most essential of what we are is probably in art.
Art is, in one way, a perfect complement to man's quest for wisdom. André Comte-Sponville even tells us " Shakespeare, Rembrandt or Beethoven have enlightened us more, about man and the world, than most of our scientists. Art as a reflection and a sublimation of our creation is also in great upheaval. Our technologies and our sciences have offered it new perspectives and new fields to investigate. Apparent limits have been erased and the beauty of creation touches the miraculous.

We find in the work *micrologus,* the way in which music took on meaning from the sound of hammers. Science and art are then found in the discovery of Pythagoras that we have mentioned through his laws: "A certain Pythagoras, a great philosopher, travelling for adventure, came to a workshop where they struck an anvil with five hammers. Astonished at the pleasant harmony they produced, our philosopher approached and, believing at first that the quality of sound and harmony resided in the different hands, he interchanged the hammers. This done, each hammer retained its own sound. After removing one that was dissonant, he weighed the others and, admirably, by the grace of God, the first weighed twelve, the second nine, the third eight, the fourth six of some unit of weight. He thus knew that the science of music resided in the proportion and the ratio of numbers. What more can I say? By putting in order the notes according to the intervals mentioned above, the illustrious Pythagoras was the first to develop the monochord. As it is not lasciviousness that one finds there, but a rapid revelation of the birth of our art, it met a general assent among the scientists. And this art has gradually asserted itself by developing to this day..." [55]

Section summary

Man is caught up in a paradox of time where he seems to belong to a present, despite himself, which only offers him furtive images of the past. He is seated in the middle of a moving present, like a symbol of the instability carried by his environment, but also by himself. In a quest for stability and to cross time and space, he offered himself a quest, a power. This power is that of building knowledge capable of enduring and of explaining what is most unknowable in the world: the universe, what it is made of and the laws that apply to it.

In this exercise of understanding and creating a shared resource, man will have recourse to metaphors of different kinds. The first is scientific. The one which represents the world with numbers, with symbols, with equations. This metaphor is extraordinarily accurate, which continues to surprise us. However, the great book of nature remains forever incomplete. Another more colorful and artistic metaphor is that of myth. This myth is the reflection of a belief and not of an absolute truth, but it carries with it a perceptible reality.

The two metaphors complement each other and offer man a wealth of interpretation and understanding of the world that appeals to thinkers, scientists, philosophers and artists. They are however fragile and carry paradoxes. How can order arise from disorder? How can an error generate a progression? How does the myth reflect reality? How can a science be a distorted form of knowledge?

Language is a strong symbol. It evolves with men, with technologies. It even disappears at times. This primary metaphor of meaning sets a trap for us. That of no longer looking for the essence at the heart of things but prefering their superficial sense.

It is interesting to note that we have natural symbols of artefacts capable of transcending time. It is now the objective of science to continue to contribute to knowledge and its preservation, that of safeguarding our heritage. This heritage is both the code and the message sent to the universe through who we are, what constitutes life and DNA. An ark is envisaged, it must allow us to survive and give meaning to our species beyond ourselves. Technologies make it possible to dream about it, to dream of knowledge that goes beyond our humanity, knowledge that is not simply lost in the hands of a fragile being. Knowledge that can be reduced to the atom without disappearing.

Caught up in this technological momentum, we forget our fragility, but also everything we do not know. However, all the sciences show how gigantic a space is always in front of us, waiting to be discovered. This position of ignorance pushes us to continue our quest.

In the midst of our representations, what place should we offer to the digital and technological world? Is it simply a tool for sharing and memorizing? Can it change our perception of reality as far as our own reality? Physicists wonder about the possibility of a universe whose fundamental building blocks are information. Can we then see the emergence of a joining of the physical, digital and abstract world under this unity? The manipulation of life, the manipulation of atoms, the creation of quantum computers, and artificial intelligence offer us avenues for reflection and action. *Homo sapiens* seems to be about to find a new freedom and a unique opportunity to think of and understand the world. This freedom passes by a new way of expressing and conceiving our art. Art, this inexhaustible vector of expression constitutes the continuation of our quest.

The new artists

Where art crosses certain limits including those of life and time. It takes on a new body with technology, nature and artificial intelligences.

"From now on, the role of the artist will no longer be to create a
work, but to create creation. "
Nicolas schöffer

FIRST CHAPTER

An eternal sun

When our old companion illuminates our arts.

There will always be a sun to host a day, whether it is sad, difficult, joyful, the first or the last of our lives. There will always be a sun. As wrote Louis Aragon, there will always be a first dawn... The sun is still 4,603 billion years old. He is older than every wonder we can discover around us, and for which he is partly responsible. He is like an immutable landmark of our lives, and yet constantly in motion. All the impulses of this world, microscopic and macroscopic, make us see things stand still before our eyes. From quantum in motion and in uncertainty, to our fixed objects, our reference points are regular. The sun is one of those immutable benchmarks despite its permanent rotation. It is this same, faithful companion who shed light on the battles of the Greeks, those of the Romans, the constructions of the seven wonders, of which he saw six collapsed. He is the one who accompanied and warmed the silver reflections of the sea. The one who cradled the first forms of life, molluscs, algae, fish, reptiles, insects, dinosaurs, birds, dolphins, dogs, cats and of course primates. Finally, primates, who have become artists, know what they owe him. He is the precious collaborator of many artists. Precious to the point of giving him privileged access to their workshops, their houses with large windows to allow him to express himself and allow them to express themselves. Leonardo da Vinci insisted on light and on its role in artistic creation: "Sculpture first requires a certain light, that is to say a light from above, and painting takes its light everywhere with it. and its shadow; sculpture owes its importance to light and shade. " [56]

He saw the birth of all the works of all humans and so much more. He arose on the days when life had no meaning, no existence, he will rise on the days when life no longer has any meaning. He was there that simple and banal day of 2018. A day spent in the lowlands of Gosier in Guadeloupe. That autumn morning, his rays warmed me, and the Coereba flaveola (birds of the order Passeriformes) came to scrape sugar around my coffee. He had something to do with it, at that precise moment when my heart felt happy. Happy to belong to this moment in time and on this tiny piece of land. Land whose patience and fidelity must be blessed. This messenger of happiness does us unparalleled good.

Figure 11: The god of Sun, Aton, with hands on the world of ancient Egypt. Akhenaten achieved the feat of propelling the Sun to the rank of a religion, henotheism (Figure 11).

What makes us want to live and create above all, I believe, is the Sun. What could be more normal? We owe him our possibility of living, located at an ideal distance from the Earth which allows him to to give us life. A few tiny variations in this distance would have condemned all forms of life, reducing to nothing any reason to contemplate it. Finally, a miracle among miracles, when he hides, he gives way to a starry sky. A sky that opens a door to infinity. A journey through time and space. A celestial image which is perhaps the only one that has not evolved in the eyes of men for millennia. It offers itself to us at night with as much ease as it did in the Jurassic area. If there is one thing that men of all ages have contemplated, the sun, the stars.

He is only one star among billions, but he has this uniqueness, he exists in the eyes of beings who think and dream. In the eyes of a creative and imaginative species, aware, if we can be, of its place at the heart of billions of billions of galaxies, themselves with billions of stars. This is what makes him great. An opening into a space that seemed limitless and borderless to him. This search for freedom carries art and does not constrain it. However, our digitalization raises the question of barriers, these frameworks which, although virtual, impact on our works.

CHAPTER II
Think creation outside the box
Where it is a question of algorithmic boxes.

Thanks to computer systems, everything is now sold and delivered in boxes. Information, culture, a film, an image, a love. All its boxes shape us to their images, and only we shape them too little to our own. The image is built of those that are placed, without too much hassle and without some errors, in the same box, the same segment. By algorithms, loyalty cards, stolen data, in any case captured. No computer program will have qualms about doing this, pushing you down the path that appears to be yours, and forming impassable walls for you in other directions. The stake is economic, because uncertainty is the enemy of conversion, that which leads to the almost automated act of purchase of our minds. Behind the apparent disorder of the web hides again an order. It is economics. *Homo sapiens* has become a number, translated into a matrix, a probability, a vector, a network, often simply a point in a multidimensional space. A space like a support easy to calculate, to mathematize, to put into equations. A way to create proximity between behaviors, to find trends and to inject ourselves into a planned or measured trajectory. Round, polygonal, rectangular, square or more complex, the box is present in the head's manmade algorithms.

Isn't our Google search engine holding back the creative process? What uniqueness to extract from a world where everything stops at the same content seen and highlighted through an exploration window, the browser? We take the same paths, the same roads. We discover them through the same looks, the same eyes. Sorting the observable is antithetical to creation. We forget to look and seek the source and the nature of us. Creating the order of disorder can be akin to a style but creating an art of the same common order can present a risk. The temptation to reproduce the seen and the known can become a brake at a time when this "seen" and this "known" is offered by algorithmic engines which offer us their vision of the world. In the book *Urban watercolor sketching* [58] the author rightly reflects that it would perhaps be necessary not to search in order to find.

The artist has finally succeeded in the improbable task of finding his style and even more incredible of imposing it, but doesn't this style too often become a new form of servitude, an ease of doing the same at the origin of a loss of creativity? Having a style offers the possibility of having one's works recognized by the public. Going out of this style is often badly perceived by an audience waiting for this imprint. The specialists reproached François Mauriac for writing with the same style and on the same subjects. He explained himself by replying: "It's a curse. As soon as I write something, it's Mauriac." The style is essential to the artist, who is himself its author. Creativity, however, teaches us to think outside the traditional framework. Albert Einstein summed up his thinking by saying: "To invent is to think sideways. A desire to innovate which is not quite understood by the machine. Also, it will have great difficulty integrating it into its system. Maybe that's what can still save man. We who know the importance of art so well have never created so many boxes. Is it therefore easier to think outside? When they are in the millions, in the billions, I do not believe it. Jean d'Ormesson insisted on this power: "Invaded by science, overwhelmed by images and advertising, we dream, we paint, we write, we think of something else or nothing with less and less freshness and more in addition to artifice."

And yet, the variety of our works, just like their beauty, is staggering. Works are created by robots, others partially burnt by their creators, some dissolve to the rhythm of drops of acid which fall on blocks of limestone. Canvases are painted from the back, writing mirrored, tiny pots painted from the inside with a single-haired brush. Some works are ephemeral, spectacular and self-destructing, others, architectural, have been unwavering for millennia. Some are drawn, others written, danced, sung, viewed, picked, collected. Noisy or silent, visible or invisible, major or minor, they come in all colors and shapes, of all natures and of all eras.

Some creators go so far as to transform themselves into cyborgs. One of them Stelios Arcadiou (Stelarc) wills to surpass the body to illustrate there (?) are limits. He has invented a third arm to complete the work of the other two. In a desire to show the obsolescence of the human body, in 2007 he had an ear grafted on his arm. This initially had sensors to record sounds that would eventually be removed due to infection. He wanted to show that you can go beyond the limits of your body for listening, imagining technologies to transmit sounds from body to body. His exploration of the body and its limits in connection with technology would take the form of a dance in his work *Ping Body*. One way of alerting us to the control that information flows can have over men. In this work, his body is connected to the internet and to a set of sensors controlling movement. Internet users can then send signals to control it. We perceive it to be dancing chaotically. Only his articulated third arm is supposed to remain under the artist's control (though this does not appear to be the case). This is an image that could challenge and highlight the body like a technological puppet. The artist denies this desire and indicates that he wants to show that technology is a vector of modification and acceleration of the body. It is precisely located in between the virtual body and the material body and illustrates the complex interactions that can exist between the two.

If technique accompanies and enables art to evolve, it remains only a means. The essential remains in the ideas that are conveyed, and the testimonies brought to us.

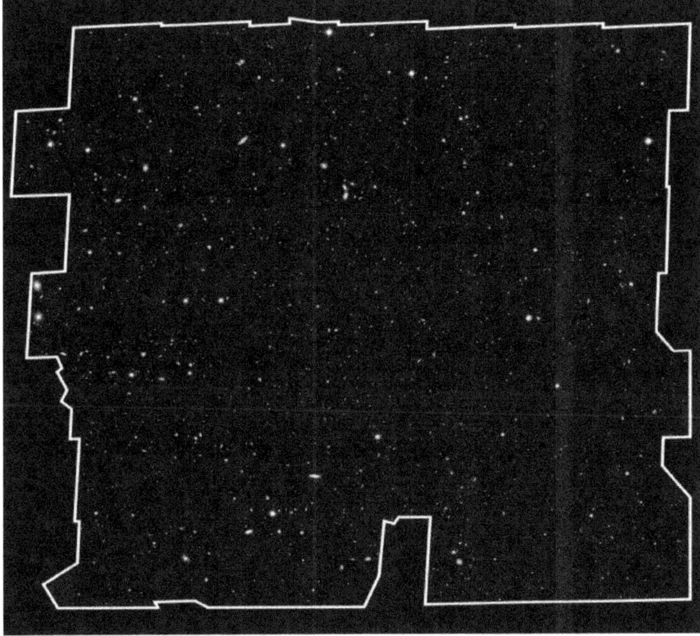

Figure 12: The Hubble Legacy Field image represents a very small portion of space observed e for more than 16 years by the Hubble space telescope. This image dates back 13 billion years.

The work, if there is one, which is the most incredible of all is the one in which we are all embarked. The one in which all the other works live. This universe is monumental. I believe above all in creative beauty and in the creation of beauty. The photo of distant stars and galaxies captured by the Hubble Space Telescope is the result of more than 16 years of observation. We are surrounded by this gigantic, dynamic, creative and majestic work, a cosmos created with aesthetics and elegance. This unique work goes beyond the simple passers-by that we are (Figure 12).

The passerby is no longer surprised by the everyday things. Placing ourselves in boxes, formal or informal, psychological or material tarnishes our view of this marvelous design. It tarnishes our life and reduces our contribution to this genesis. Art escapes from the boxes without losing its codes. Emotion carries art more than its origin. Whether man or artificial intelligence is the designer of the work, the two complement and sublimate each other.

Works of art are mirrors of time and of the soul. In this sense, they enlighten us. The upheavals we are commenting on are expressed and rediscovered through art. It reflects our questions, our concerns, our epoch. Its richness offers us its beauty and an additional dimension of discovery to our challenges: a glimpse of its future and ours, a view of our technology and tools. It is a dimension that marks us and stands out from the ordinary to make us act and react better. Is art unique to man? Hegel taught us that it is the soul of the artist that is reflected in his work. If artificial intelligence produces works of art, what soul can we hope to find there? A mixture of what other artists' souls have produced and which is restored by their aggregation, or simply a work without a soul? Is the lack of creative soul equivalent to a lack of emotions? Could we believe in a designer soul indirectly present behind the algorithm at the origin of the work? Would this intermediary erase the artist or would it sublimate him? Is art the bridge between man and superman?

Our journey into an artistic universe shaken up by the machine begins with coup 36. A work that is positioned as a reflection on the place of man in relation to technology.

CHAPTER III
Shot 36
Or art sublimates the doubt of artificial intelligence.

Here is a story that will speak to chess players, as well as to machines that will certainly remember it. A rare moment transcribed as follows in algebraic notation.

1.e4 e5 2.Nf3 Nc6 3.Bb5 a6 4.Ba4 Nf6 5.0-0 Be7 6.Re1 b5 7.Bb3 d6 8.c3 0-0 9.h3 h6 10.d4 Re8 11.Nbd2 Bf8 12.Nf1 Bd7 13.Ng3 Na5 14.Bc2 c5 15.b3 Nc6 16.d5 Ne7 17.Be3 Ng6 18.Qd2 Nh7 19.a4 Nh4 20.Nxh4 Qxh4 21.Qe2 Qd8 22.b4 Qc7 23.Rec1 c4 24.Ra3 Rec8 25. Rca1 Qd8 26.f4 Nf6 27.fxe5 dxe5 28.Qf1 Ne8 29.Qf2 Nd6 30.Bb6 Qe8 31.R3a2 Be7 32.Bc5 Bf8 33.Nf5 Bxf5 34.exf5 f6 35.Bxd6 Bxd6 36.axb5 axbx5 372B 38.Qxa2 Qd7 39.Qa7 Rc7 40.Qb6 Rb7 41.Ra8 + Kf7 42.Qa6 Qc7 43.Qc6 Qb6 + 44.Kf1 Rb8 45.Ra6 1–0

Phenomenal!

An explanation is in order. We are in 1997, the human World champion of the game of chess, Garry Kasparov, for the second consecutive year faces the supercomputer Deep Blue. A duel of two geniuses which spanned two confrontations. On the one hand, the supercomputer capable of evaluating 200 million positions in a second. On the other, the Russian international master and first player to have exceeded 2,800 Elo points in 1990. The Russian champion was coming out of a first clash he won 4-2 in 1996. A year later, the duel between the man and the machine will become legendary. Will the machine take its revenge?

The part that interests us here is the second game of the confrontation. It has something special: the move 36 played by the machine. A surprising shot from Deep Blue. A move that does not seem to be the result of a calculation, but rather of a human strategist.

36.axb5

Instead of a logical, mid-term gratification move, the machine will surprise us. It's making a subtle and strategic decision that will pay off in the long run. Garry Kasparov, surprised, will announce: "I understood on February 10, 1996 at 4:45 pm that I was facing a form of artificial intelligence ". Not reassuring for the grand master, rather stunned by this audacity. That year, Kasparov will lose the match, but also and above all the confrontation. A singular moment in the history of chess and artificial intelligence. A fight that some have qualified as unequal. The human champion was fighting with a brain whose energy consumption is around 20 to 40 watts. Next to Deep Blue was a machine of incomparable power that consumed ridiculously more energy.

This moment inspired a work of art, that of Eduardo Kac. The description of his work is drawn in figure 13. He presents a chessboard made of earth and white sand in the middle of an empty room. There are no pieces on the board. On the other hand, positioned exactly where Deep Blue made its movement 36, stands a rather peculiar plant illuminated by a light beam. The plant has been genetically modified. Its genome incorporates a gene created specifically for the work. This gene uses the ASCII code (a computer standard for coding characters) to represent René Descartes' famous statement: "Cogito ergo sum" in the four bases of genetics. The symbols are powerful and mix playing with genetics, life, intelligence, nature and a moment in our history. The gene allows the leaves to be curved, which characterizes the presence of the modification. It represents a way of confronting man with his creations and of asking the question of the limit that the machine can reach: "I think therefore I am" as a border between our lives and our creations. A symbolic work of art. The artist explains: "The presence of this Cartesian gene in the plant rooted precisely where humans have given way to the machine, reveals the fine line between humanity, inanimate objects with characteristics close to life, and organisms. Living organisms that contain digitally encoded information. "

Figure 13: Coup 36, the work of Eduardo Kac.

Finally, the famous move 36 will lose its miracle. The IBM engineers announce that it was just a bug in the program. A creative bug, was it possible? A bug that looks like a man. Finally, it is when the machine derails that it appears more human. After all, some see dreams as a dysfunction of our brain.

Following move 36, man's next challenge will introduce move 37, in an entirely different clash 19 years later. This new confrontation is that of Lee Sedol with AlphaGo in the complex and strategic game of Go. A game whose number of possibilities could drown the most advanced algorithms, and where creativity and strategy are essential. This move 37 is that of AlphaGo which will take place during the second confrontation. It will be commented on by specialists as a creative and unique move. This movement will surprise the best players on the planet and will destabilize the champion, Lee Sedol. He will admit to having been beaten psychologically, more than technically. This creativity in the machine and algorithm will open up a new avenue of strategic reflection to human players, now inspired by the machine. Garry Kasparov will react to the game with the following remarks marking the person-machine duel of the new era: "Computers excel at perfect calculations; our brains, generally speaking, at long-term planning and the application of general models to new situations. This contrast produces exciting clashes in those short windows of time where men and machines play on equal terms, as was the case in chess twenty years ago and apparently in Go today."

Like the bug, creativity is often thought of as unpredictable. However, once the artist's path has been taken, could it be captured and predictable to the point of being reproducible and equaled? Can we do the same with an already created universe, even if its artist is iconic and uncertain? Would it be possible to put everything into an equation, including art?

Can we believe in a mastery of all the laws of nature? Can we imagine the limits that man might reach? Are they fictitious or real? If this is possible (it seems impossible currently because of the number of elements to analyze and our calculation limits), the associated power becomes unacceptable. The mathematician and physicist Pierre-Simon Laplace described the situation as follows: "An intelligence which, at a given moment, would know all the forces with which nature is animated, the respective position of the beings which compose it, if moreover it was large enough to submit this data to analysis, would embrace in the same formula the motions of the largest bodies in the Universe, and those of the lightest atom. Nothing would be uncertain for it, and both the future and the past would be present to it. "

Can we witness the disappearance of *homo sapiens* to see the appearance of a posthuman who will carry within him a form of humanity? If our flesh is taken from us or our consciousness is copied or downloaded into the machine, will we still be able to have some form of humanity? In large part, what creates man is his social relations and his interaction with the environment. What forms of creativity can be hoped for in a digital and digital nature?

Can creativity be reduced to finding patterns in data? This question leads to the question of man's monopoly on being creative. Can the machine be creative? Is consciousness necessary to produce a work? Can the machine supplant man in his creative capability?

To date, it seems that it can at least imitate man in this task. This is what it has already accomplished on the piano.

CHAPTER IV
The deep blues of music
Where artificial intelligence plays with our sensitive chords.

Artificial intelligence began its career in an imitation game, the famous Alan Turing test. A test where it had to appear human during an interrogation in front of a human. A little later, it faced the greatest chess masters. Phenomenal duels leading to a victory against world champion Garry Kasparov. We reproached this intelligence for over-calculating and lacking in strategy. With a burst of pride, it learned to master the game of Go, a more complex game. it won again and beat the grandmasters. Then, tired of only learning in human footsteps, it ended up moving forward on its own. A small step for the machine, but a big step for artificial intelligence. It started to confront itself: playing alone against itself on the basis of simple rules and without additional knowledge. By learning from its mistakes, it improves its performance. In each new game, it faces an improved and richer version of its defeats. In this cycle, it will end up playing the game of Go excellently (AlphaGo then AlphaGo Zero). A unique and superhuman feat, but ultimately not more than a game. Some still laugh, because it seems play more than work. Criticism is easy, from "game" to "I", there is not much distance. From now on, the intelligent machine becomes slightly Artistic.

After playing comedy for Turing's pleasure, in music artificial intelligence works wonders. It can listen, not to be moved but to react and turn the pages of a score at the convenience of the musicians. It can grasp the sense of rhythm and accompany a soloist with percussion instruments. An artificial intelligence that no one questions when it is a slave. But what happens if we touch the characteristic of man that is emotion?

What capacity would it have to interpret the scores of the great classics? How can we even get closer? To allow an artificial intelligence such a feat, it will have to learn to play in style and not like a vulgar computer from another era. This rhythm, it can be learned, at least it can be studied. The pianists each have their specificities and the machine has a homogeneous and regular rhythm, which is not a source of harmony or emotion for our acute human ear.

The beauty of musical expression comes from pauses, silences, rhythmicity and improvised timelessness. Dimensions which are intangible and not indicated on the sheet music. By studying the performances of great pianists on thousands of scores, the machine has identified trends. Subtle variations on certain precise sequences which are reproduced by the greatest artists. These variations, once tamed, can allow it to deliver an inspired and almost systematic interpretation of these artists. The *deep blues* of music would happen in 2018. After having conquered in logic, an artistic path would be conquered.

A panel of people were subjected to the musical Turing test. Who could recognize a professional artist, a naive machine, an interpretation performed with artificial intelligence algorithms? The famous study published in the *Journal of new music research* shows that humans are duped by the interpretation of the machine. Unable to distinguish who the artist is. The *deep blues* (in reference to *deep blue* and the musical genre) are proclaimed and artificial intelligence will have an artistic future. The authors claim that algorithm-generated piano music may be identical to human performance. We draw a parallel here with the victory of the *Deep Blue* supercomputer in chess. It would seem, however, that a discerning ear would be better able to distinguish the subtleties and not be fooled so easily, at least for now.

What will remain of the musicians' expression? I liked to think that an emotion carried by the genius of Frédéric Chopin, Ludwig Van Beethoven or Wolfgang Amadeus Mozart would never be grasped by some forms of machines and artificial intelligences. Today, the distinction is not so obvious. The music, the canvases, the images have become partly artificial. The analysis of writing is another area where the digital seems to thwart historical limits.

CHAPTER V

A writing that binds to who we are
Where artificial intelligence psychoanalyzes the author.

I tested with interest one of our best artificial intelligences, that of Watson by IBM. Its name pays homage to Thomas J. Watson who was president of IBM from 1914 to 1956. This intelligence has recently discovered an almost artistic talent for psychoanalyzing the human from his writings. It echoes, more than 50 years later, the first Eliza chatbot, imagined by Joseph Weissenbaum. In 1966, he imagined a text robot capable of (roughly) imitating the work of a psychiatrist. In 2020, its successor is called *Personality Insights*. Let's not be fooled, the objectives are marketing. Its purpose is to get as close as possible to the human brain without having to read its waves or connect it to a machine. To predict our behavior, our preferences, our weaknesses, our emotions better, in order to satisfy us better, with the goal of relentless consumption. A valuable tool for automating mass consultations and without the knowledge, of course, of the psychoanalyst. The textual traces left by billions of social media users are an important resource for fueling our financial machine. Our research, our messages, our communications, our everyday words are invited to this exercise. *Personality Insight* reads as follows: "Predict personality characteristics, needs and values through written text. Understand the habits and preferences of your customers on an individual level and at scale."

Far from pecuniary considerations, intrigued, with barely hidden enthusiasm I throw myself at the opportunity to do my analysis. Will I smile again at the result, like my personal assistant who often does not understand much? It is usual to be rather disappointed by the broken promises of this type of intelligence. The connected speakers left a funny feeling with their not very poetic refrains: "Sorry, that doesn't ring a bell", "Sorry, I can't answer your request". Will I be surprised at the depth of the result? I am transmitting in full the prelude to the work *digital prison*. Good or bad, I offered it something important, something genuine. If Paul Valérie affirmed that he was not always of his opinion, this text had asked me for time and I was rather of my opinion. I send the text, Watson analyzes it, analyzes me, I suppose, and answers me in the language of Shakespeare, which I translated into the language of Molière: "You are insightful and strict. You challenge authority: you prefer to challenge authority and traditional values to help bring about positive change. You are philosophical: you are open and intrigued by new ideas and like to explore them. You are independent: you have a strong desire to have time for yourself. Your choices are motivated by a desire for discovery. You are relatively indifferent to both tradition and the pleasure of living. You care more about making your own path than following what others have done. And you prefer activities whose purpose is greater than simple personal enjoyment."

I can hardly believe it. A small piece of text allowed him to understand my almost obsessive quest for freedom.

This will to exist.
To be, so as not to be in the crowd
To be, so as not to be directed
To be what I simply am
At a time when this is no longer taken for granted.

These unalterable ambitions which have always caused me difficulties. He seems to see it so right from almost nothing, from a few words. I am reassured that I have not transmitted the entire book to him. Who knows what artificial intelligence would have made of me?

The fear of finding myself there to the point of losing myself there.
The fear of being imprisoned by my own digital prison.
The fear of being absorbed into the machine.

So I stay quietly.
One word knows what we are.
One word is who I am.
What I am pursuing.
I.

Intelligence foils the man from his texts, confronts him in logic and interprets classics brilliantly. It is also possible to observe his new exploits in painting. Let us say welcome to the inceptionism and the ganism of artistic movements on the computer.

CHAPTER VI
A canvas by AlgorIthme
Where artificial intelligence begins to paint.

In images, ganism and inceptionism are two generative artistic movements carried by machines and algorithms. Their creators hide behind artificial intelligence, as if to allow it the 'premiere' of the opening, to embellish the surprise and to make the simple dreamer dream.

Ganism originates from the artificial intelligence technique abbreviated as GAN for *Generative Adversarial Networks*. These artificial neural networks compete in turn to achieve excellence. As a way to artificially simulate the neural plasticity of our human brains, the network adjusts the weights between its artificial neurons. It is this plasticity which in humans makes it possible to adjust the quantities of neurotransmitters in order to improve the quality of the transfer of information, of electrical signals. Changes that are the source of memory and learning. Each of the networks consecutively tries to do better than the others, until all become extremely skilled. In a way, like many algorithms and some humans, they learn from their mistakes. The works produced, you will understand, are artificial. Some parameters still belong to the human creator, even if this is actually no longer necessary. The works are generated and self-generated without being defined in advance, without even the designer knowing exactly what he is going to produce.

An art which is self-generated in the image of life, which occurs and is self-produced. The nucleobases are pixels, Men are the color pigments which form the human canvas. They arrange themselves, rearrange themselves to give them a new life, a new color.

A double thunderclap struck the artistic world when the Edmond de Belamy canvas (Figure 14) was sold for over $ 400,000 by Christies. It was the first piece of artificial intelligence to be sold at auction. It is signed with an equation, as if to recall the computerized nature of the work and its algorithm.

Figure 14: Canvas produced by artificial intelligence called: Edmond de Belamy. This work draws on more than 15,000 classic portraits of the XV ᵗʰ to the XIX ᵗʰ century.

Inceptionism (or neuron-art) is a similar movement whose name was suggested by Google when launching a panoply of spooky images on the web. The name of this movement would be inspired by the film directed in 2010 by Christopher Nolan *Inception*. This momentum offers us images of an artificial intelligence dreaming. An example is shown in Figure 15. The artistic current launched by *Deep Dream* again comes from a network of artificial neurons. The latter, usually able to recognize shapes on the art images, are used to make an art generator. Starting from a random image, the process forces the network to create an image corresponding to learned objects. These objects are repeatedly emphasized in order to give them existence in the final rendering, even if their presence is not at all evident in the original image. The initial image is often a mere noise. The work seems imagined or hallucinated by the network. It is a new way of creating aesthetic order from disorder: a form of pareidolia. We experienced it when we were younger, when we had fun looking for shapes in clouds. As adults, we still use that creative talent, but for more serious things like Hermann Rorschach's inkblot test.

If psychoanalyzing an artificial intelligence does not make much sense for the moment, making it observe objects has allowed us to discover a remarkable artistic power. A similarity even seems found between the art works produced and some hallucinations experienced by humans in drug taking. Jeff Clune, assistant professor of computer science at the University of Wyoming opens a lead: "The fact that humans report that Google's inceptionism looks like what they see when hallucinating with LSD or other drugs suggests that our brain machinery is similar in some way to deep (artificial) neural networks. " [66] Another ray of light on the similarities observed between digital and human natures. Our investigation is progressing.

Figure 15: Inceptionist image produced by the Deep Dream software.

If surprising works are produced ex nihilo by artificial intelligence, can we program the machine to capture and reproduce the style of the greatest artists? Could we give birth to a new Van Gogh or a new Rembrandt?

CHAPTER VII
Capturing a style
Where artificial intelligence impresses us.

In the tradition of artificial intelligences imitating the famous Turing, the machine has recently taken a new step: imitating a great master such as Van Gogh or Rembrandt. Do the works The Red Vine, The Olive Trees, Café Terrace in the Evening, Mauve Souvenirs, Self-portraits, The Starry Night contain all of the master's ingredients? Hours, days, months and years to transcribe and produce an imprint, a style, an emotion in the paintings. Would it be possible to sum this up in equations in a few hours? Equations expressed as a result of the works and no longer as a creative process.

The question is not naive. The universe is the most complete, the most complex work. However, our sciences have never ceased to express this universe in equations, and this, with rather astonishing success. Life is not a simple work, and yet once again, we have grasped a few features: in equations, chemical relations too. Our sciences have always had as the supreme ambition finding the right models, the right laws, the right equations and, if possible, the right equation. Albert Einstein refused political responsibilities to stay with them. He freely admitted the reasons for his choice, he found them something more eternal, out of time. If the genius of Stephen Hawking continued to hope or fear any theory at all, here is a quote from *The Brief History of* Time [67] : "I think there is a good chance that the study of the early Universe and the demands of mathematical logic will lead us to a completely unified theory during the lifetime of some of those around us today."

Could a mathematical equation that can explain the universe cover all of man's creations or just the life around us? Do our inspirations derive from that first equation? Life is more like a code than an equation, an already well-known genetic code. It makes us who we are. Are we then doing what we are encoded to do?

Creators have often used mathematics and some form of logic to design their arts. We remember the music of Johann Sebastian Bach and his use of symmetry. The talent of Leonardo da Vinci and the famous Vitruvian man which derives from an artistic, anatomical, geometric and mathematical miracle, that of making a perfect man fit in a circle, but also in a square with perfect, balanced and aesthetic proportions. To understand the feat, you have to listen to the master explain it: "Nature has distributed the measurements of the human body like this: four fingers make a palm, and four palms make a foot, six palms make an elbow, four elbows make the height of a man. And four elbows make a double step, and twenty-four palms make a man." He used these measures in his constructions. If you open your legs to lower your height by a fourteenth and extend your arms so that your fingertips are level with the crown of your head, you should know that the center of your extended limbs will be at the navel, and that the space between your legs will be an equilateral triangle. The length of a man's outstretched arms is equal to his height. From the hairline to the bottom of the chin, there is a tenth of the height of a man. From the bottom of the chin to the top of the head, is an eighth. From the top of the chest to the top of the head, there is a sixth; from the top of the chest to the hairline: a seventh. From the nipples to the top of the head, is a quarter of the height of the man. The greatest shoulder width is contained in a man's quarter. From the elbow to the end of the hand is a quarter. From the elbow to the armpit, it's an eighth. The full hand is one tenth of the man. The birth of the virile member is in the middle. The foot is one seventh of the man. From the sole of the foot to below the knee, is a quarter of the man. From below the knee to the beginning of the genitals, is also a quarter of the man. The distances from the bottom of the chin to the nose, and from the roots of the hair to the eyebrows are the same, as well as the ear: one third of the face. [68] "

But can we go the other way? Reduce works to equations, reduce artists symbols, reduce a style to numbers? This unique imprint of a man, this flavor that only he can bring to his creations, which allows him to stand out and be remarkable? Our intuition is challenged by the greatest minds in the quest for demystification, one of the universal quests of science. Could we, more than 350 years after the loss of Rembrandt's talent, produce a new work inspired by his style? The *the next Rembrandt* project attempted the adventure: giving life to this artist's soul through artificial intelligence. Ron Augustus describes the project with an interesting parallel: "We use technology and data like Rembrandt used brushes and paint for his canvases to create something new. A database containing the collection of the artist's paintings had to be established. Three-dimensional scans, analysis of images, colors, shapes. Oriented towards the question of the characters' emotions, the artificially generated work would logically be a portrait. Its specificities would be taken from the artist's style: comparison of faces, their characteristics, respect for proportions and colors. Ultimately, *the Next Rembrandt* project [69] enabled the production of what one might call a new Rembrandt.

The work presented in Figure 16 offers many reflections on our relationship between art and technology.

Figure 16: Work produced by an artificial intelligence having learned in the style of Rembrandt.

Another example is offered by employees of Cambridge Consultant who found the equations of the genius Vincent, precisely the name of their machine to produce a Van Gogh [70]. An intelligence capable of finishing your sketches into a Van Gogh facsimile. The result lets us believe it, and that is perhaps the most important, the most impressive. Creation goes beyond the works, goes beyond the artist, creation has no other support than its own limits. Other artists will soon also be matrixed, filter matrices that may one day find a place on social networks.

Would a great master have recognized his style? Would he have stopped painting under the anger of seeing his talent captured or stolen by the machine? In the game of Go, the champion Lee Sedol ended his career in 2019. A decision motivated by his defeat by artificial intelligence, and the feeling of never being able to dominate his discipline.

When the machine has learned from our greatest artists, will it give way to novelty? Should authors be worried about seeing the emergence of a new work by Louis Aragon, Marcel Proust, Plato, Aristotle or Chateaubriand, every year, every month, every day, every second? What place will be left for novelty?

What place should be given to an imperfect man combined with the future?
Should we strive for artistic perfection?
Can this subjective art please all subjects?
At all times?
Should I hope to see the verb on my pages transformed into a great author's text?
Should we continue to write the old-fashioned way with the fear of not being fair?
The fear of already belonging to an outdated fashion.
More than ever, the risk is to not please.
That of transforming us into a more than perfect human in search of perfection.
Artificial intelligence is putting its feet on the mountain of creativity.
Man will have to face the limit of the authentic and the creative.
There will be no simple future for artists.

Technologies have offered us screens as a new vector for our creations, a vector whose medium is almost intangible. What remains of the material?

CHAPTER VIII
Works without support s
Where digital makes us lose the support of art.

The elders will understand the importance of matter in creation. It reassures, it even obeys us most of the time. It allows us to manipulate it, to fold it, to cover it, to cut it, to transform it, to pierce it, to strike it, to make it vibrate. It allows us to moisten it. We do this with pleasure, but with taste by adding pigments to make the exercise more joyful and colorful. This matter is common sense that which does not create disagreement. I have a sheet of paper under my pen and everyone by my side can confirm that. If I don't like it, I roll it into a ball, it obeys me, and I throw it away. As simple as that, I feel what I write about the material, it follows well-mastered rules, rules that give me the impression of creating. I perceive the words given form by my ink. I see the page filling up as I write. All this has meaning, has the meaning, that of time, of matter. Finally, common sense.

Man has looked everywhere around him for support for creation. When he had no more papyrus, plants or fabrics to express himself, he could still write and draw on the ground and in stone.

In our digital works, there is a problem. We produce sketches without molecules, arts, whose material and support are elusive, files whose place of conservation is unknown, and documents that we struggle to keep for more than 30 years. If digital work does not forget anything and memorizes everything, it only seems to be for a short time. Files disappear, data is lost in the network and instantaneity. Digital technologies are not the best recourse to overcome the fear of being erased and of losing our works. Our mastery of the living allows the impossible, reading and writing our art and our scores in living things. Nature now dictates her art.

CHAPTER IX
When nature dictates its art
Where we discover the partition of nature.

Can a musical work be based on a reading of nature? It is not a question of a reading as a painter, an author can do, a reading as an interpretation of what is offered to our eyes and to our hearts. This is a nanoscopic reading taken on a simple and surprising organic object. To find it, you have to cross dimensions and reduce yourself to the scale of the invisible. Cross the spaces, from man to a cell, but even smaller, from the cell to a bacterium, and further reduce from the bacterium to the viroid, a particle whose size is measured in nucleotides. There are 250 to 400, and each is no more than a third of a nanometer. This viral particle is made up of a single circular RNA strand. This strand contains information. If it does not encode any protein, for the pianist, it might encode an interesting score.

Jörg Schäffer has been leading this investigation since the 1980s. After all, Gottfried Wilhelm Leibniz, philosopher and mathematician used to talk about music as an exercise in secret arithmetic. He claimed that whoever engages in it is unaware that he handles numbers. Enriched by this teaching, Jörg Schäffer relies on and with nature. His objective is to scrutinize the sequence of bases in search of harmonious melodies. By observing his notes, we discover a series of nucleic bases marked with the four characteristic letters. Some are highlighted in yellow; others are striped or finally surrounded. The meeting and the search for natural harmony between the infinitely small and an artist takes place. The encounter of a pathology with our pathos. The etymology gives it this double meaning: from an illness to a touching hyperbole. The result is a 30-minute piano solo. I had already appreciated Nature's moonlight, its seasons, its air. This time, I discovered her music. Was it by nature musical? Have we made this musical nature? Is it inspirational or a deciphered message: melodious or organic? Organically inspired or melodic? It seems that both are possible.

We store the Arecibo signal, a radio message sent into space in 1974. A signal transmitted at a frequency of 2380 MHz and modulated by shifting the frequency by 10 Hz, with a power of 450 kW. 210 bytes in total which encode in wave form an image representing man and life. The signal continues on its way towards the globular cluster M13. It will reach it in 22,000 years. If it has no real hope of one day meeting a listener, an audience, let's imagine this all the same. We may assume that for an artist the one who receives the message would find an image there. This alien could pass for a mad if he discovered the binary digits, the components of DNA, the nucleotides and even the double helix. Even more surprising if he also recognized the image of humanity and a solar system. This is, however, the information it contains (Figure 17).

Music and RNA are a surprising encounter. Jörg Schäffer, over the years, has extended his work to many other forms. Some of the compositions are inspired by the amino acid sequence of glutathione-S-transferase from Schistosoma japonicum, but also from the famous C. Elegans. One work is even inspired by the atomic spectrum of hydrogen and helium during the nuclear fusion of the Sun. Music that has never been more aptly inspired by nature and our old star. Perhaps one day our works will no longer be written and bound to synthetic, steel or gut strings, but rather to strings located at the very heart of the material.

In his reference work, Douglas Richard Hofstadter [73] the professor of cognitive sciences and computer science, but also professor of philosophy of science, had highlighted the intimate relationship between nature, life and art. He saw the process of protein biosynthesis as a musical metaphor. Proteins, ribosomes, and the message r RNA are seen as a triptych as in music. The ribosome would be the recorder, the messenger RNA a cassette and the synthesized protein the music. The functional metaphor is appealing: "When a strand of mRNA, after leaking from the cytoplasm, encounters a ribosome, a complex and beautiful process called translation takes place. We can say that this translating process is at the very heart of life, and there are a lot of mysteries associated with it. But in essence, it's easy to describe. Imagine that the mRNA looks like a long piece of a magnetic recording tape, and the ribosome could be a tape recorder. As the tape passes through the recorder's playhead, it is read and converted to music or other sounds. Thus, the magnetic marks are translated into notes. Likewise, when a strip of mRNA passes under the playhead of a ribosome, the notes that are produced are amino acids, and the pieces of music they make are proteins. This is precisely what translation is."

A complex and almost perfect musical biology, a harmony in a process which allows life, and which takes place every moment in our body, a rhythmicity, a rescue and a transfer of information. Beyond giving us life, it is a factory to keep us alive, a machine whose smallest mode of operation dictates solutions to major problems. How to keep information going? DNA is the winner. But also, a machine which by its mechanics, unconsciously pushes us to love the beautiful, naming what is beautiful without being able or having to define it. A machine that allows us to recognize a work of art universally and without discussion. A beauty that is usually so subjective suddenly becomes objective in the eyes of all and gives life to the object. The amphitheater of Leptis Magna, the Mona Lisa, Nympheas, Valley of the Kings, the Acropolis, the temples of Angkor, the cave of Lascaux, the Sistine Chapel, the pyramids, the mountains, the sea, the S oleil are works that amaze everyone, go beyond our differences, our tastes and our characters. We cannot disagree on the beauty of nature, of life and of man.

Art is a field that came to life on the biological scale. New creators are now qualified as bio artists.

CHAPTER X
Bio Artists
Where art lives and where art lives.

Art is a field that has never set limits. We have seen it by photons, heard it in waves, touched and sculpted it. We danced it, we wrote and read it, we even erected it as a monument to symbolize its importance. However, it is not surprising that it is taking a new direction. This direction is driven by the desire to get closer to living things and matter. The possibilities offered by biotechnology have allowed a new generation of artists to emerge. These bio artists [74] our contemporaries draw with a new tool, life, the living, in new workshops: our laboratories. They express themselves with brushes on new, clearly perceptible media. The brush is often invisible, but the medium is alive.

An example of a creation that could be called artistic is that of screens made of bacteria. These replace pixels to display a message. The bio artists are researchers from the University of Texas at Austin and the University of California at San Francisco. They managed to display the phrase "Hello everyone!" with this living system. E. coli bacteria programmed to detect and respond to light. To quote their words, this is made possible by using a protein domain of cyanobacteria to control the lacZ gene, which can cleave a molecule to produce a black pigment.

In the millennia of works, we have many examples defying the possibilities and the usual limits. Biocouture is the project of generating clothes from living organisms. Growing clothes is therefore possible. Biomaterials emerge as a promise for the future. Jen Keane has developed a microbial weaving process. It relies on a modification of the growth of the bacteria k.rhaeticus to create fibers. The fiber obtained is exceptionally strong.

It is possible to breed leather with mushrooms. Even if we knew since Lavoisier that nothing is lost, nothing is created, everything is transformed, these new combinations are surprising. BioCouture Research Director Suzanne Lee grows clothes in the same way as seeds germinate. She uses fermented kombucha tea to create tissue. A mixture containing bacteria, yeasts and other microorganisms allow it to obtain cellulose fibers by an environmentally friendly and natural process. A very haute couture art that finds its meaning in the face of the challenges we face.

We cannot speak of art without mentioning one of its most attractive forms: poetry. William Shakespeare defined it as music that every man carries within himself. Can it reinvent itself to enter a new technological era? What if this progression allowed the symbol of an unparalleled longevity for a poem recited by nature?

CHAPTER XI
Poetry recited by nature
Where nature tells us a poem.

Some poems have passed through the ages, worn by wise men and learned by children. We all have the memory of a forgotten poem whose verses come back to us from a few words. A poem mastered by our souls as kids. Those who remember them recite the verses like a memory of yesteryear that belonged to them, as if to go back in time and relive the naive moment of a child's recitation by heart. A little forgotten, but intact, a poem had marked me in this way. A single verse by Victor Hugo, from the collection *Les Contemplations,* which calls to me and reminds me of all the others. Timeless, the words are still there, they have not aged.

> Tomorrow, at dawn, when the countryside
> turns white, I will leave. You see, I know you are waiting for me.
> I will go through the forest; I will go across the mountains.
> I cannot stay away from you any longer.

> I will walk with my eyes fixed on my thoughts,
> Without seeing anything outside, without hearing any noise,
> Alone, stranger, back bent, hands crossed,
> Sad, and the day for me will be like the night.

> I will neither look at the gold of the evening, which is falling,
> Nor the sails in the distance descending towards Harfleur,
> And when I arrive, I will put on your grave
> A bunch of green holly and heather in bloom.

A tomorrow that will remain tomorrow. A tomorrow frozen for eternity. A poem and an author, a work among the masterpieces that will span the ages. Transmitted in writing, transmitted by sharing.

Poems recited by our hearts, rather even by life, there are now new ones. One of the most natural is offered to us by the Swedish poet Christian Bök. The poem is an exchange of verses that echoes the tragic story between Orpheus (ϱφεύς) and Eurydice (Εϱυδίκη). In the myth, Orpheus was a talented musician, handling the harp and song wonderfully. He fell head over heels in love with Eurydice, who returned that love. However, right after their marriage, Eurydice was fatally bitten by a snake. Orpheus wept for this lost love. His heartbreak was such that he decided to face the kingdom of the dead to set out to reclaim it. Thanks to his talents, he achieves the impossible, gets rid of the dog Cerberus and finds Eurydice. A condition was, however, set by the guardian of the underworld: Orpheus could leave with his love on the sole condition of never looking at her on the way home. As they had almost finished their journey, one behind the other, Orpheus turned, surprised by a cry from Eurydice. This time, he would not have another chance, he went back alone, desperate, into the realm of the living.

Christian Bök's poem offers an exchange between the two lovers. The latter is a candidate for a form of eternity. It begins simply with the words of Orpheus, son of the king of Thrace Oagger and the Muse Calliope:

<u>*Orpheus*</u>: *Any style of life is prim*

The project of this work is enormous: to have it recited by nature. For that, we must have recourse to genetic information, that of DNA. This first worm will be encoded in the DNA of a living bacterium. Nucleotides are used as a code to represent the letters of the alphabet. An encoding like we do in binary language for modern computing. However, when the cell of this organism multiplies, Bök wishes to allow it to encode in its RNA a response, an echo: the voice of Eurydice. A biological poem, like a mirror of love. The rest of this verse is issued by a process at the heart of life. Nevertheless, nature has its constraints. We cannot infer the process and the poem must follow a compatible logic. The enzyme (Eurydice) must respond without errors to Orpheus, even if we know that the RNA which encodes the gene is closely linked to the DNA. We cannot make Mother Nature say what we want. To bring the poem to life, the two voices which are linked, the artist must ensure that the letters used are mutually transposable, in accordance with the biological process imposed by his tracing. The complementarity of the bases.

From paper to life, each support sets constraints, limits, from an edge of a sheet or canvas, from the hardness of a material to be carved, to the melody of life, to its chemistry, we cannot turn away from the atom. Christian Bök is here constrained by a bijective substitution process. The appearance of an E in the first line will be irremediably linked to the appearance of a Y in the second and vice versa. It is the same for all the other letters and for the whole of the poem. If each letter has its mirror, each word has its image. Thus, the word *always* (Any) will be systematically translated by *the* (The). To accomplish such a technical and poetic feat, the vocabulary is reduced. You have to think of words in transposable pairs. Helped by a computer program, Christian Bök has built a panel of eligible words, a dictionary of possibilities. He continued to work on his goal even after 15 years of effort and more than a hundred thousand dollars spent in this dream. Getting a poem to recite a poem to life is not easy. Finally, his bet was announced to be successful in 2011. The poetic code, the X-P13 gene, did indeed cause the E. coli bacteria to change color to phosphorescent red. This means that once implanted in the genome of this bacterium, the first line of the poem all life is first gets a response, an echo.

<u>Eurydice:</u> The faery is rosy of glow

The constraints are respected, and the mission is successful. Nature is becoming more poetic than ever. We can dedicate this feat to all those who thought that there was no poetic embarrassment, a snub to those who did not believe. The poem in question remains the major work, even if the technique and the associated ambition are are without comparison in history. To try to grasp part of its meaning, we have to observe it in its totality and like a game of metamorphosis between Orpheus and Eurydice who respond to each other by transforming themselves.

The translation is offered for information only, as it cannot be faithful nor equivalent to the original. Studies of this poem and its meaning have been contributed by many authors. Some of the most striking elements have been detailed in David Ferrier's book. Here is what is suggested about the artistic will of the work. A parallel is proposed by the exchanges between the two lovers as a criticism and a concern on the meaning of life in the face of genetic engineering. While the metaphor is not obvious, the term " lyre " seems to be used as a symbol of genetic engineering. It is corroborated by the expression "rosy of glow" which is used in reference to the fluorescent color produced by the *mCherry* protein which is used in genetic engineering to make the transcriptions visible. This is precisely the one that allowed Bök to be able to announce the success of its operation. The entanglement of the terms " rosy " and " life " brings an eye on life and its artificial modifications. The parallel turns to a concern clearly expressed in Orpheus' songs of lamentation.

He moans his fate linked to the loss of Eurydice. Possibly linked to the loss of (eternal?) Life and that of the beauty carried by the rose. A precious detail is illuminated by the study of Ferrier which specifies that the use of the expression "in fate we rely", "we depend on our destiny" would refer to the sentence of the geneticist and biochemist James Dewey Watson about the *Human Genome* project. This project launched in 1988 and led to the complete sequencing of the human genome after more than 15 years of work. He said: "We used to think that our destiny was in the stars, we now think that it is in the genes."

Orpheus   **Eurydice**

Orpheus	Eurydice
Any style of life is prim	The faery is rosy of glow
Oh, stay my lyre	In fate we rely
With wily ploys	moan the riff
Moan more grief	with any loss
The riff	Any loss
Of any tune aloud	Is the achy trick
Moan now my fate	With him we stay
In fate we rely	Oh stay my lyre
My myth	We wean
Now is the word	Him of any milk
The word of life	Any milk is rosy

This new life-modifying art could be a precursor to sorrow as stated in the chain "with cunning ploys" and "moan more sorrow with any loss". The fragility of our species is recounted, and destiny perceived as a painful fate, mourning the end. The author concludes the analysis of the poem: " Thanks to Eurydice de Bök, the bacterium protests against the painful thing imposed on it. [...] This should not be read literally, but laterally - from the particular to the general, also protesting against the broader regimes of violence that lead to extinction. The dread of the celebration of biogenetic potential is therefore a much darker recognition of the violence inherent in these projects and in multi-specific relationships in general. "

It is the mise en abyme of a poetic work in abyss. In this project, transmitting through life is not a guarantee of transmitting for life. To succeed in this quest, Bök considers the help of D. radiodurans. This bacterium is one of the most resistant in the world. It can survive extreme temperatures, a vacuum, acid, radiation, as well as dehydration. It can resuscitate itself. A few hours after its death, it can come back to life by repairing her DNA. Far from the sheets of crumpled paper, such a support at work offers a dream of eternity for a poetry more fragile than ever.

CHAPTER XII
A living art to reinvent our role
When to write while alive is a new art.

If art has never been an imitation of nature, if natural beauty is not artistic beauty, if we are constantly erasing borders and reshuffling the cards, do we still have to distinguish between art and nature? Man has achieved a mastery of life and the infinitely small which is not natural, but which is worthy of a work of art. What if nature now dictates an art form to us? Maybe you just needed the tools to hear it, to understand it. Life could become a medium of art after having been a metaphor for so long. As we have seen, the support can be a living one. The support is alive. The living is support. The artist rewrites fragments of life.

We understand the dangerous game we risk. By wanting to make the fate of living beings aesthetic, we can divert it from its functional beauty. Removing the sense of the functional or losing it to the detriment of the beautiful can destabilize nature. In between, artists with genetic brushes (they are often scissors [85]) and with microscopic eyes offer us a sublime look at a technology of all dangers. Man seized his chance; he gradually enriched the specter of what falls under his control.

We saw him measure time,
Fight to win,
Measure distances,
Fight to find out,
Then conquer the lands,
Build opinions,
To fight for them,
Create works,
Fight to keep them.

He will have loved, he will have killed, he will have controlled fire, invented tools, hunting, art, writing, agriculture, science. Above all, he will have always survived and lived. On this earth, he will have known how to pass and surpass himself. At one time, we saw him fly into space, further than ever, higher than us, as if to refuse his fate as an earthling. Yet throughout his history and all these stories, there was one thing we did he'd never seen done. No one had ever seen him write the living, invent it, synthesize it or manipulate it. This is not a simple and banal power of death; it is a much more powerful and dangerous power. It is the power of life. That of the writing of life, of the alteration of life.

If we stick to the artistic dimension, is it ethical to grant oneself the power to rewrite genetic material for a simple aesthetic desire? Man is already a work, a natural product. He is certainly one of the masterpieces among the works, the result of an evolution made possible by nature, its laws and perhaps a certain chance, a creative will and certainly survival. It is both the work and its result. He has acquired the power to at least partially dominate his software, his genetic heritage, and those of certain living beings who surround him. Is he recreating himself in an artistic impulse? Little by little, he will have muddied the waters and broken the codes. To this day, digital and organic natures are losing their differences and their duality.

It seems more than ever that
The whole takes on the meaning of one
And it all has a meaning.

CHAPTER XIII
From art to nature
Where art and nature meet.

Man is made up of and surrounded by a multitude of simply fascinating forms of life. Plankton, the phytoplankton to which we owe a good part of our oxygen. The saxifrage pyramida, the Welwitschia mirabilis, the Rhynchostruthus, the naked mole rat - symbol of resistance, the Beatragus hunteri, the Gecko, Turritopsis nutricula in the power of a fairy and so many others are part of this, are of life. Over a trillion species that are active at every moment, with more or less discretion. Day and night, in every corner of this old earth, life is there and it's incredible. So much life that a large part is even still unknown to us and a majority totally imperceptible and inaccessible. A surprising modesty of our time, a time when the earth is bugged and where we claim omniscience through big data.

Our existence, in addition to being stuck in the vice of time, finds itself locked between an infinitely small and an infinitely large, between a gigantic past and an uncertain future. Man is condemned to observe this wonder with his simple eyes and through a reduced angle of this infinity of possibilities. For a moment and without artefacts, he will capture his inspiration from what surrounds him, from nature and the world in a present that is slipping away. For the rest, he will use an effort of imagination and abstraction to make it a reason.

When in his mirror he sees double, man offers us odes to love, words chosen in a sublime order, flashes of beauty and love that he could not find otherwise. Louis Aragon will have sublimated the eyes of Elsa, Pierre de Ronsard, Alphonse de Lamartine and so many others will have sung the beauty of love in a double. Bök even gave life to Orpheus and Eurydice.

Nature as an art is remarkable
At all scales and at all times
If I have any doubts about his future
It retains many mysteries today
That we can only observe conditional
We reveal some of its secrets
In the continuation of our imperfect course.

Section Summary

Technology opens new doors for our artistic expressions. If art had never set limits, it was nevertheless a victim of what we cannot imagine, what we cannot live, what we cannot manipulate, of what we cannot create.

The sun was the preferred companion of artists over the centuries and millennia. Technology has given us a new sun, a new way of observing the world, to represent it, to think, a new hour watch face. We have moved from an Anthropocene era to an Algorithmocene era. The latter tends to confine us, while art has never ceased to seek a free expression and often out of the frame.

Can a machine think outside its own frame? This is what move 36 will teach us, or more precisely, will lead us to believe. Artificial intelligence has spawned an artistic way in many areas. It has opened a track in music and learned to play it, but also in writing where it learns to analyze and almost psychoanalyze. It is even making progress in painting, where it imitates styles and produces new works of dead artists.

The technologies seem to bring works without support where creation is stored as bits of unknown essence, existence, and the temporal and spatial livelihood.

Finally, could nature be a new medium? A new source of inspiration on a scale never studied before. We read music in sheet music while we were alive. We wrote our scores and our texts in the living. We have used the living to create art. We have even had a poem recited by the work of nature.

The joining of art, technology and life offers an unparalleled look at our power, our weaknesses and our hopes. A look at the end of organic and digital borders, a look at what is gradually becoming the new nature of man. In the rest of our quest, let's explore this nature. Let us remember these marvels and their relationship to man. We may then be able to understand the content of the possible better. The paths that digital nature can take.

From digital and organic nature

Where organic and digital nature mix and merge, for better and for worse.

"A quiet revolution is underway. It occurs under the microscope, on a molecular scale, far from our daily lives. A new genre of designers is inspired by biology and bionics to rethink our world by re-orchestrating our relationship with nature."

thisisalife.com

FIRST CHAPTER
A wonder
Where nature is wasting away while remaining silent.

In his famous *discourse on the method,* René Descartes explains the need to make the human species the master and owner of nature, in particular in the quest for better health. A phrase that echoes many of our current debates. If it is utopian to consider that progress would only bring men wisdom, it is important to note that this does not mean being master and possessor of nature. The intellectual mastery mentioned therefore refers to a better understanding of its mode of operation, in order the better to understand our place and to anticipate the challenges of a humanity with growing technological power. The philosopher specifies[86] : "To make ourselves the masters and owners of nature. This is not only to be desired for the invention of an infinity of artifices, which would make it possible to enjoy the fruits of the earth and all the conveniences which are there without any difficulty, but mainly for the preservation of health, which is undoubtedly the first good and the foundation of all the other goods of this life. Even the mind depends so strongly on the temperament and the disposition of the organs of the body, that, if it is possible to find some means which will generally make men wiser and more skillful than they have been hitherto I think it is in medicine that we should look for it."

Today, this nature is suffering. The report[87] living planet of the WWF (Worldwide Fund for Nature), established in partnership with the Zoological Society of London, informs us of the growing degradation of our ecosystems. The famous Living Planet Index (LPI) indicated in 2018 a drop of 60 % in just over forty years in some 16,000 populations, representing 4,000 species. A sinister expression of the pressures we exert on the planet.

Although the philosopher Michel Serres had already proposed a natural contract over 30 years ago, it was finally heard only very recently.. This contract proposed completing the social contract by adding a human contract with nature. A proposal which still remains valid, in particular with the envisaged modifications of the French constitution in order to underline the importance of this debate. Its urgency is felt both by natural observation and by the emergence of technologies which offer man the power of modification and the massive destruction of nature, of which he himself is a part as beneficiary and victim. Nevertheless, who cannot marvel at such a richness even if it has partly disappeared. It is all the more cruel that in this disappearance, it seems even more beautiful to us. Like a memory that begins to fade, and that we try to revive in our memory whenever the opportunity arises. Imagine for a single moment all the species of this planet in front of you. They would be frozen at that precise moment. A representative of each species would stand there: a n elephant, a giraffe, a wolf, a bacterium, a whale, a parakeet, a clownfish, a snake, a caterpillar, a kangaroo, an otter, a koala, a cat, a crustacean, a panda… All gathered to show you a tiny sample of the variety of life. With all their differences, their sizes, their complexity, their beauty, their colors, they delight us, touch us, frighten us, amaze us, nourish us, educate us.

Science has long debated the astonishing clarity and simplicity of Charles Darwin's grand theory of evolution. How to achieve a form of life as complex as man on the basis of selection and mutation? How can we imagine that all of humanity descends from a common ancestor? A theory that will explain to us the obvious paradox of life. Life forms look alike at the same time as they are different. The resemblance is borne by the common origin of the species, and is observed through the almost insane universality of DNA, present in all forms of life and at the same time carrying all the difference in its unity. Variety as an effect of time and of the modifications that have taken place in the course of history and of species, branches that have been created and have gradually led to a thinking and unique form of life that is *homo sapiens*. The tree is the symbol, if any, of life, origin, species and knowledge. A significant sentence would be pronounced by the geneticist Theodosius Dobzhansky: " Nothing makes sense in biology except in the light of the Theory of evolution. The three observations that led to the most important theory in the history of biology are as follows. The characteristics of the species vary and appear to be inherited from generation to generation. A population can produce many more offspring than can survive. This allows for natural competition. And finally, the species seem particularly well adapted to their environment."

The theory maintains that individuals whose hereditary traits are better suited to the local environment are more likely to survive. They are more apt to reproduce than less well-adapted individuals. An idea that was inspired by the observation of different forms of beaks of finches on the Galapagos islands particularly suitable to their environments. Over time and over generations, there would be an increasing proportion of individuals who possess beneficial characteristics. Evolution occurs as the uneven reproductive success of individuals leads to adaptation. This is how nature can contain secrets, illegible at first glance, but which dictate its work. She will have learned over time, a time inaccessible on the scale of a man, rules and remarkable adaptations. Observing nature brings us a glimpse of the sensitive past, which has become, over the ages, an intelligent and fragile present.

Are all these forms of life the result of chance, spontaneity and adaptation to a function? Living beings have such a remarkable practical aesthetic, it's hardly believable. Their existence is a blessed gift from heaven, chance or necessity, just like ours.

Nature has spoiled us with millions of species of which we observe and know only a tiny part.

Can we understand the complexity of what surrounds us?
The physics that make things happen
And makes them what they are
Myths that make up what beliefs are
And makes them what they are
The words that make languages
And makes them what they are
So many unanswered questions
So many unknown questions
The world has this wonder
Until we grasp its complexity
It will keep something magical, pious
Something that seems in the hands of a creator
This incomprehensible something that makes sense
That something that makes us forget the how
Which allows us to travel in beauty
And to dream our reality
Every day of eternity

One of the few things I'm pretty sure we won't grasp soon is the complexity of this world, of this nature. We can therefore dream in peace Neither science, nor religion, nor mythology offers a satisfactory and exhaustive explanation of this reality. Nor of other existential questions: of death, of the past and of our future. So,

Every day when I wake up, I marvel
The impossible seems to always be possible
The inconceivable seems to be conceived
The unimaginable was imagined
The improbable has taken place
We are here
You are there

Both feet anchored on the earth, placed by gravity, assembled by atoms and well-accommodated hydrogen bonds, maintained by strong interaction, informed by our DNA, intelligent as our matter can allow us to be and as alive as we can claim to be. Isn't there some gravity in coming to terms with this intelligent matter from which we hold life? So much energy, in one place, in an instant, that then leaves and vanishes. This energy is a chance, it is our chance. It allows you to contemplate the nature that is offered to us in a ray of sunshine.

Technology has shrunk distances, opened human eyes to the greatness of the world and its wonders. Friedrich Nietzsche, having devoted many works to art, would be the first to grant nature artistic sense: "Artistic forces spring from nature itself without the mediation of the artist and by which nature finds to satisfy primarily and directly her artistic impulses. The artist has the duty to transcend this work in order to sublimate it."

Let's continue our journey in search of these works of nature. In this quest, science and technology have obviously enabled us to uncover some secrets. Will they answer our questions?

CHAPTER II

Hidden wonders of the planet

Where the author discovers our planet from a new perspective.

Man digitizes. He probes, he tracks, he memorizes everything in his path. He catches this reality which he locks in digital boxes as if better to give it the impression of existing. Perhaps this is a good sign for our effort of memory? The technologies allow the capture of data and events using two main types of sensors of variable reliability and performance. On the one hand, physical sensors: probes, microscopes, telescopes, cameras, satellites, smartphones, magnetic resonance imaging, magnetometers, etc. On the other, a sensor born with digital technology: humans. Accompanied by an acolyte called, somewhat wrongly, a smart phone, man tracks down his environment and reproduces it in blogs, photo libraries, tweets, messages on networks. He offers the result of this snapshot to the web giants (e.g., Google, Facebook) who store all this preciously.

Cameras embedded on the roof of the *Google Car* enabled the digitization of all the roads on the planet. Satellites have been doing painstaking work for years in search of the smallest piece of land and asphalt to digitize. Some satellites are able to read the newspaper over our shoulder. They provide a hitherto inaccessible image of the planet. If that's scary, let's take a look at the discoveries that make us happy. We have been able to discover new lands, unexplored places, a gold mine for knowledge. Among the new finds, the so-called *Spinning Island* visible in Figure 18, discovered in Argentina thanks to *Google Earth* images traveled by Sergio Neuspiller, producer and director of films in search of a filming location. This singularity, discovered in 2016, is a disc floating in a circular lake, like an eye. Its center moves every day, which gives the impression of coming to life. A little eye of our planet.

Another fascinating discovery is that of the largest natural Arch with a height of 120 meters identified in 2010 by Jay Wilbur of the *Natural Arch and Bridge Society* (NABS) using satellite images. It is located in Xianren in the Guanxi Autonomous Region of China.

In 2011, scientists found Egypt's hidden treasures through analysis of infrared images from a NASA satellite. In total, 17 pyramids and several thousand tombs and houses have been identified. They had been buried under the sand for millennia, hidden and as if protected by nature. In 2020, some of these gems rose from the ground. The fifty-six sarcophagi discovered in the single region of Saqqara call us to order. The wonders of this world are not only in the infinitely small nor in the infinitely large. They are sometimes hidden under our feet. Sometimes they are even hidden within us. But we will have the opportunity to come back to this.

I remember a visit to a forum before a walk to the famous Blue Mountains near Sydney in Australia. Color that we owe to the gasoline produced by eucalyptus forests and which is emitted in the air. A walker announced that he had found traces of unlisted Aboriginal engravings. Hidden under vegetation and camouflaged by trees, the discovery was confirmed by scientists. Here again, our means of communication and location have something to do with it. This ability to see more clearly, further, through matter is a source of memory: from memory to discovery.

We, who see smaller than ever, further than ever.
We, who have securely attached our planispheres to the walls of schools,
like a frozen image of this world.
We, who wrote and printed our history and listed our species
Years of collections, museums, encyclopedias and phylogenetic trees like
immutable observations.
We, who have digitized our knowledge and our planet.
We, who have the power to destroy everything.
We can still be amazed by the unknown and the new.
We still have so much to discover and invent.

Like Saqqara, quantum, brain, underwater fumaroles where life might still be being born, the planet has subtly hidden certain treasures from us, as if not to reveal them too quickly. It only makes them accessible to the thread of patience, science, wisdom and progress. It quietly continues to create new ones at the rate of seconds, days, years, centuries and sometimes millennia. There remain countless unseen and unseen wonders, lost treasures that reappear and bring us back to our dreams of exploring an unknown and wonderful world to travel.

If the planet is the same, age has too often taken away our childhood dreams. I do not know if this is wisdom. It seems to me that it takes place in wonder. After all, the most immutable thing we keep from the child to the old man is our eyes, our gaze. It doesn't seem to get older over time. It is identical to offering us a wonder that cannot be tarnished.

I like to think that if man continues all these efforts to discover the hidden secrets of our planet, it is, at the end of his adventure, to understand that he owes it everything. By observing it closely, it shares some of its secrets with us.

CHAPTER III
A lesson in natural aesthetics
Where nature tries to explain its beauty to us.

Nature inspires moments of truth to those who will take the time to contemplate and understand it. From a flying bird to a blooming flower, from a disappearing cloud to a flying butterfly, all seems wisdom. Nature is a reflection of our trials, our fears, our successes and our hopes. She brings lessons, fables worth counting. She also has a certain mathematical elegance that we discover through symmetry, laws and sometimes numbers.

The French have happy hearts. We can measure it in the light of our unfailing optimism and in the face of a simple daisy that we strip with simplicity and certainly a touch of cruelty. Our heart offers us a song of hope: "he loves me, a little, a lot, passionately, madly (more than anything), not at all, he loves me, a little, a lot, etc. ". On the other side of the Atlantic, the ritornello is less poetic and more hazardous: "He loves me, he doesn't love me, he loves me, he doesn't love me, etc." ". Nothing will take away this romanticism from the French. What fate will the last petal reserve? A dreamed imagination, a real hope or a sad disillusionment.

Daisies have been scrutinized by scientists who sought in them some form of response to universal beauty. A search for ordered structures (Figure 19). Would a simple count of the number of petals of this pearl be enough to reveal its mystery? Let's watch it closely. The stamens at the heart of our daisies form spirals. Very often the same number: 21 in the clockwise direction and 34 in the anticlockwise direction. Let us add that these daisies often have 21 petals.

Pinecones, when viewed from the back often have 13 spirals in the clockwise direction and 8 in the anticlockwise direction. The heart of the sunflower has 34 direct and 21 indirect spirals. We can continue. The spirals of the cabbage are 8 in the direct direction and 5 in the indirect direction. On its astonishing version, the Romanesco has 8 direct and 13 indirect spirals. All of this is romantic, but maybe not at first glance.

The mathematician and founder of accounting, Luca Pacioli, saw it as an ideal fallen from the sky. To be convinced of this, we have to rely on the famous Italian mathematician Leonardo Fibonacci. The latter has developed a series of figures. This sequence can be obtained by adding together, successively and to infinity, the two preceding numbers of the sequence. Trivially, the first two chosen will be 0 and 1. The values are then calculated with ease and elegance 1 (0 + 1); 2 (1 + 1); 3 (2 + 1); 5 (3 + 2); 8 (5 + 3); 13 (5 + 8); 21 (13 + 8); 34 (21 + 13), etc. Those natural numbers which are in some way associated with metals, belong to this list.

Stopping there would not solve the mystery. If not belonging to the same list of numbers, what would all these numbers have in common? Precisely, a number: the golden ratio.

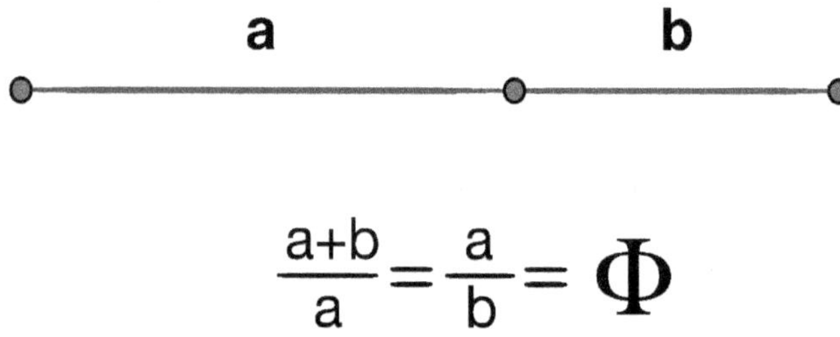

$$\frac{a+b}{a} = \frac{a}{b} = \Phi$$

Figure 20: Mathematical and geometric representation of the perfect proportion.

This number is the Phi (φ) which makes it possible to obtain a perfect ratio between the whole and the part. The master builder of the Parthenon in Athens does not count for nothing in our history. Phidias is the author of the third wonder of the world, the chryselephantine Zeus. A wonder that disappeared in a fire in Constantinople in 461. His other wonder, the Parthenon, displays many links with this number.

Consider two segments, one large denoted a, and one small denoted b (see Figure 20). The total segment is of size $a + b$. For a perfect ratio, a perfect proportion, we look for the value that allows us to obtain the same ratio of the large segment (a) to the small (b) as that of the total segment ($a + b$) to the large segment (a). Euclid expressed it as such in *Book VI of the Elements* : "A line is said to be cut in extreme and average reason when the entire length relative to the largest segment has the same ratio as the largest to the smallest"

Mathematics allows us to establish the calculation by simplifying the equation considering a reference segment length 1. Under this condition, $b = 1 - a$ and the system has only one unknown $x^2 = x + 1$. The positive solution retained corresponds to the golden ratio $\frac{1+\sqrt{5}}{2}$. The one that beautifully harmonizes the relation of the whole to the part: 1.618. We can note that two consecutive elements of the sequence when divided one by the other approach this number. This observation is all the more correct as one advances in the Fibonacci sequence. For the conclusion of this mathematical lesson, it will be necessary to analyze the size of the leaves. You will then discover that these are often inscribed in golden proportions: as a rectangle, a spiral or just a golden number. This irrational, metallic number is so natural. Observe with a fine and calculating eye the leaf of the fig tree, following the example of the daisies, you will perhaps find the same continuation and discover the divine proportion there.

Observations of this number have continued to increase over time in nature (at least in appearance), always with the doubt of its absolute truth sought by humans. In the case of plants, however, we end up being convinced of this. A model of the arrangement of leaves on a stem has been proposed, we're talking about phyllotaxis. This model helps to explain how the observation of the golden ratio is possible. It is the cause of a growth mechanism of the stem which consists of developing the organs one after the other, while respecting a space between them to allow them to ensure optimal development. It is mainly the result of an inhibitor that will prevent the development of organs that are too close to each other. The mathematical model has shown a link with the golden ratio. The summary of the contribution is convincing and one of the best indisputable links demonstrated to date between nature and the golden ratio. The researchers tell us: "A specific crystal order, involving the Fibonacci series, has so far only been observed in plants. Here, these patterns are obtained both in a physics laboratory experiment and in a numerical simulation. They result from self-organization in an iterative process. They are selected as a function of a single parameter describing the successive appearance of new elements and the initial conditions. The order is explained by the tendency of the system to avoid periodic rational organization, leading to convergence towards the golden mean. A self-organizing smart form of life who gave us the golden ratio. Its meaning is rather simple, a periodic organization of the leaves on the stem at the time of its growth would have led to the latter being stacked one under the other. Under such conditions, only the tallest leaves have privileged access to the sun, to light. The others could not have achieved suitable growth. In observation, the leaves interfere as little as possible to promote optimal distribution on the stem and maximize access to light. This development was necessary."

Is it because we are looking for this number and want to see it that we are measuring it? Does it exist outside our mind? This question is as complex as that of consciousness, intelligence, or reality. Is its existence justified outside of our desire? Anyway, it advocates an aestheticism of nature. This gold proportion was even called the divine proportion by the monk Mathematician Fra (Brother) Luca Pacioli, writing in 1498. What we cannot doubt is its use by man. Even if it only had a truth in our heads, we have built objects inspired by it, and which give it an undeniable reality. A belief that impacts reality, and that anthropologists know well. A credit card, a sheet of paper, a National Geographic logo, Apple logo or even website interfaces. Its reality is now anchored by nature or by belief.

Finally, we discovered an intriguing link between the size of the skulls of primate species and the number of gold (the nasioiniac arch divided by the parieto-occipital arch and the parieto-occipital arch divided by the frontal arch). It has been shown by researchers at Johns-Hopkins University that the dimension of the ratios of the skulls gets closer and closer to the golden ratio depending on the sophistication of the species. Surprisingly, like a prophecy, humans occupy the place closest to phi (φ). Researchers believe this discovery could have important anthropological and evolutionary implications.

Has our species converged towards some form of ideal: excellence, optimum, beauty? A form that allows us to create the most sophisticated technologies. Is it to achieve a goal? One last goal? Once again, questions are piling up and answers are scarce.

If nature has found the usefulness of aesthetics, it also teaches us a form of serenity and a new look at our relationship to time.

CHAPTER IV
A nature that looks like truth
From the wisdom of trees.

What a pleasure to bring to you the blue color of our sky or the light of distant stars from our past. A nature so beautiful and so right that it inspires us with a form of truth. We also find it through trees. They mark our time while going beyond our scale of existence. In this they surpass us and represent a form of philosophy.

The old cedar of Lebanon brought from England by Bernard de Jussieu in 1734 to the Parisian botanical garden stood there proudly during the French Revolution. Today, he is still there to observe with curiosity our modern manifestations. He will have greeted our great-grandparents and experienced a period of history which is unknown to all of us, or, at least, only known through words and stories lived by proxy. This phase of our timescales seems indisputable, reassuring and a vector of happiness. As a last of its supernatural powers, the wisdom carried by nature seems to be transmitted to the walker. A modest dreamer, fallen from the sky in an era, without having chosen it.

Much older than the cedar of Lebanon, we know that some trees can live for thousands of years. This is the case of the surprising Bristlecone Methuselah pine (Figure 21). We find it at over 3000 meters in the heart of the White Mountains California. This pine tree is named (Methuselah) in homage to the oldest character mentioned in the Old Testament, who died at the age of 969 and was finally quite young compared to the age of the representatives of his species. The oldest, Prometheus (Προμηθεύς), was estimated by dendrochronology to be over 5000 years old. Unfortunately cut, by necessity or by chance, as part of a scientific study on the subject. You will certainly meet on your way, and not so far from your home, cedars from another era. Under their branches, much more modest plants will dot the ground. Although they offer you flowers, they will die out quickly in the eyes of the giant. It's like an impossible fable, similar to Orpheus and Eurydice. If a friendship was born between the two species, it would never last more than a few springs. This bond which would bind the two specimens would, each new year, be as strong as the ephemeral specimen. Faced with this pure friendship, so new and fragile, each year, the cedar could only open its heart. Each cycle would mark the end of this love. One would be frozen in a form of eternity and the other in a naive and lively love. One in unmade love and the other in eternal love.

Figure 21: Bristlecone Methuselah pine.

This is a situation that could be told in men's stories in the near future. If we extend our life expectancies, if we make our intelligences artificial, the emotions will not be very far behind. From a man to a superman, from a mortal to an immortal, from a mortal to a semblance of immortal, what can we hope for? Love has always been inscribed in a form of immortality thanks to the barrier of death. If this barrier were to disappear for one or the other, would love become deadly? Mortal for the one who survives and relives it every spring, immortal in the heart of the one who dies. Death is not the only one to be fragile over time, love is also fragile there. How happy we are to live in a time when love still exists.

This relationship between nature and time is also imprinted in the flesh. Carbon-14 dating is a gift that nature has given to man to measure its age. A mark of the time that has elapsed from the death of an organism and can go back up through 50,000 years of history. The presence of radioactive carbon isotopes allows this evaluation. When the organism dies, the volume of radiocarbon will only decrease, like an hourglass flowing out to keep track of the shadow of a life. A gift that is offered to us by cosmic radiation which is the marker of time. It is absorbed in very small amounts by our living organisms.

Trees, as giant as they are, are the fruit of very small seeds. A symbol, among others, of this feeling of truth coming out and taking shape in nature. Leonardo da Vinci, author of many wonders inspired by nature, correctly translated this observation: "Nature is the source of all true knowledge. It has its logic and its laws, does not produce effects without a cause and does not invent anything that is not necessary."

These observations do not stop at the organic level, since digital nature is now inspired by it. Designers understood the importance of these laws of nature to give birth and created a form of software intelligence. We perceive a facet of it with the bio-inspired computer algorithms. Evolutionary algorithms, for example, rely on a population of potential solutions to a problem to obtain the best possible options. The process will successively modify the population on the same bases as the theory of evolution. The most suitable representatives (evaluated on the basis of the desired result) will be reproduced by integrating mutations. This approach makes it possible to generate dynamic solutions adapted to the problem by following the biological approach. One track among others that allows us to trace our artificial route towards intelligence.

We are now certain, in the midst of this nature, that man has taken his place in a phenomenal and surprising way. He has become a creature apart, a creator apart.

CHAPTER V

A creature apart, a creator apart
Where man seems to modify certain rules of his nature.

Although confined to a material reality, man has regularly exceeded his limits in all areas. Today, he goes and sees further, smaller, stronger, faster. He remembers more data, longer, and perceives everything around him better than ever. The precision of his instruments continues to increase and opens a door to the microscopic and the cosmic. Homo sapiens can even decide its destiny, individual and collective. He has the power to make himself disappear in a sudden atomic reaction. He has the power to change, to change and even to send his heritage to another planet. He is a species with the power to modify his own species without having to wait for the long effects of evolution. He has made it possible for him to skip the steps.

The danger arises by destroying, from the height of this immense mastery, species which do not have this power. Our system, our research, our technology companies have made it possible to accumulate unprecedented wealth. Boredom begins by measuring its impact beyond the economy. It is curiously now in history when we best understand our planet, our species, our wealth and its fragility that we destroy it the most. An organic nature that is dying, an animal nature that we electrify to control it better, or that we end up replacing by electronic chips. Our nature is so beautiful, but its present and its future seem sad.

Luc Ferry rightly declares that nature is far from being a moral and political norm. "All the honor, not only of modern politics, but of medicine with it, lies in a bitter struggle against the natural law of selection. Our welfare systems, for example, are through and through unnatural, built against the elimination of the weak. Whereas biological nature is anything but a moral and political norm. Sometimes there is some good in it, but it's up to us to decide, sort it out, and choose what we want to keep or throw out of it. " [96] Nature obviously offers us reflections in multiple directions. The American physicist Frank Wilczek reminds us that the physical world embodies beauty, but it also houses misery, suffering and conflict. In any of these aspects we must not forget the other. If not all directions of nature are acceptable for humans, many reflections inspire us and dictate to us a doctrine that deserves reflection.

Whether we advocate the importance of humans on the planet or their insignificance in our cosmic history, we must agree on one thing: man has unparalleled power. In the great history, he is the first living creature to have significantly changed the face of this planet. He will have succeeded in changing its environment and disrupting the biosphere, even to the point of contributing to global warming and relegating certain living species to the stage of memory. Man has left his mark on the world in which he lives on a large scale. He is Anthropocene, he makes a whole world of what he is and of his activities, which have changed the face of our Earth. Even if scientists do not quite agree on the date marking the origin of this new era, there is no denying the evidence of a world that revolves around man. Like a return to first beliefs when our ancestors firmly believed that the Sun revolved around our planet. Geo-centrism, although comforting, has been abandoned.

A tiny, insignificant and yet symbolic reflection of our imprint is measured on the people of the air. The continued increase in noise levels in our urban areas has been felt on these avian dinosaurs. Cities are weakening the birds observed in their area. And the few species that have survived in our cities have had to adapt to our noise pollution. We see behavioral changes in birds through their songs. For example, chickadees have shortened their song in an urban environment. They sing faster, in order to increase their chance of transmitting a message in the middle of our ambient noise. The minimum frequencies of songs are often higher in large cities, to better distinguish themselves from the noises that we impose on them. This behavior reminds us of how our production of information on digital social networks has continued to accelerate as if to have even more chances of finding a hearer. Digital man is stunned by all the ambient noise of networks. Microblogging offers an interesting parallel where messages should not exceed a certain number of characters (e.g., Twitter with 280 characters). In the midst of the noise of our systems, to hear each other, we had no choice but to limit our words, sometimes even to transform them into images, to save time and to have more chance of successful communication.

This idea of a bird song adapted to its environment had been put forward in the 1970s. A study was then carried out on the differences in the spectral analysis of the recordings of birds from two distinct environments in Gabon:

the closed environments of the equatorial forest and more open environments such as the savannah. The study made it possible to show that the tonality of the songs was more serious in dense environment than in open environment. Today, we measure the impact of humans on animal behavior, and experience an impact on our communications. Let us hope that man can continue to evolve in an open environment.

CHAPTER VI

Technology as an extension of man
Where the smart phone replaces the biface in
history of evolution.

Could the telephone be an extension of modern man as the Acheulean biface was an extension of prehistoric man? This tool was used by our ancestors over 1.5 million years ago. The biface is the symbol of a breakthrough representing the impact of the tool on humans. It is thanks to this tool that *homo sapiens* was able to gain skill, which contributed to their evolution. This mastery made it possible to build new, ever more sophisticated instruments: a circle of mutual evolution.

Can this tool compare with our modern phones? If so, our future is dizzying and unthinkable. It seems that they are not comparable, at least in the role they will play in the history of our civilization. Still, they share some amazing similarities in their design and the way the two hold together in one hand. This is recalled by the image used by Apple during its presentation at the Apple Worldwide Developers Conference in 2018 (Figure 22).

In its imprint of our lives, the smartphone is undeniable. Our *homo digitalis* now holds a phone in his hand much more often than a knife or cutting tool. However, their functions differ. Should we look for the culprit of our technological dependence? On the one hand, the smartphone, the Swiss army knife of the digital world, which adapts to our needs, on the other, a tool frozen in stone. It replaces some of the functions of the body, that of converting motive power into the ability to kill, peel, carve or burn. In the modern age, our tool is, I think, at least as powerful as a simple biface. Even if it doesn't take life, it can prove to be dangerous and sharp. It might even go so far as to dematerialize man. It remains for us to hope that the latter keeps his head on his shoulders.

Throughout history, man has regularly asked himself the question of his place in relation to science and technology. Already in the last century, we imagined that each progress of cybernetics (the science which studies the mechanisms of information, communication and regulation of living beings and machines) could make man disappear a little more.

Will we soon have our heads in our hands? Like the miracle of Saint-Denis adopted by Michel Serres, the famous philosopher, historian of science and man of letters. The miracle in question is a bishop of the IIth century. The unlucky victim was beheaded on Roman orders. The miracle is as simple as it is incredible, the victim picked up his head in his hands and began to walk in the direction of the hill, as far as Montmartre. Today, although a little tortured by our technologies, we are not yet completely decapitated. However, we have in our hands, for several years now, a strange thinking animal. Smartphones, tablets, computers, watches combine the advantages of a good old -fashoioned mind: perception of things, actions, living or dead memory (like our short- and long-term memory), an ability to process, to learn with *machine learning* and *deep learning* and perhaps one day a real form of intelligence. Over time, we have personalized our devices as if to compensate for a loss. A waste of time, attention, memory, love?

We hit the moon in 1969 with ridiculously under-powered computer compared to our smartphones. We have extended the capabilities of the network and devices to make us available in real time, from anywhere in the world, at any moment.

In a nutshell: we have become ubiquitous. Having transformed memory to the largest, screens to the most miniature, then finally again to the largest, it only? remains to offer technology what it does not yet offer, intelligence: our intelligence. The telecommunication giants have investigated processors optimized for artificial intelligence. How do we know if this delegation of our primary functions is not detrimental to our development? Will it inhibit some of our brain areas? Will we develop new ones? Tools have always shaped man, just as men have shaped tools. We do not know where this semiotic circle will lead us. As our functions are delegated with more or less ease to the machine, let us try not to lose them completely from our own beings.

In this quest, I do not know whether man will reach the top of the hill or the mountain, much less what he will find if he reaches the top. From Montmartre to Olympus, the hills look alike. From Montmartre to Valhalla, the resemblance could prove tricky. In Norse mythology, it was the Valkyries who carried death among the warriors and carried them to Valhalla. Let us hope that our ambition does not lead us to the realm of the dead warriors. Let's avoid fighting each other, and let's build a symbiosis between man and machine without making ourselves either gods or slaves. If nature offers wealth to man, should we give it back in order to keep a chance of saving what took 3.5 Ga (billion) years to transmit to us: our life and humanity

Psychiatrist Serge Tisseron alerts us. The XXIst century will be that of the construction of a psychology of man confronted with machines distinct from him, but which at the same time will resemble him more and more. The complementarity of the two seems visible and possible. The machine is remarkable where man fails.

CHAPTER VII
A paradoxical future
Where man thinks his future.

In the current technological context, synergy will be increasingly necessary to obtain mutual value from the work of man and machine. On the one hand, man must take advantage of the machine for tasks at which it is more efficient than him: calculations, data storage, for example. On the other hand, humans still cannot count on machines for tasks related to social interactions or management, philosophy. To illustrate this phenomenon, let's look at the work of futurist Hans Moravec who has a photograph of human skills (Figure 23). The sea level in the foreground of the image illustrates the tasks that computers (and today's artificial intelligence) can do best. The height of the landscape expresses the estimated level of difficulty that a machine can one day acquire the skills in question. Art is cautiously left like a mountain impassable by machines, even if we have seen in this book that their march to the top is already well underway and the mountain eroded.

It is curiously when man is sensitive that the machine would no longer suffice. Moravec illustrates this through his paradox. What is most difficult in robotics is often the easiest for humans. We see illustrations of this duality in our day-to-day lives. A simple calculation is enough to lose us, a number to forget.

The machine excels in this type of task. On the other hand, the emotion so natural to man is enough to disrupt the machine. Irony is, above all, elusive to our algorithms, while humans practice it with ease. The conceptual and the spiritual are in the nature of man, the machine does not yet feel comfortable there. These are poorly managed by transistors.

The representation of Moravec is a double symbol of our modern preoccupations: on the one hand, the real rise in water levels, symbol of the climate challenge; on the other, the rise in the level of mastery of artificial intelligence, which is gradually overwhelming human skills. As the water level increases, man seems to lose his balance with the machine. The curve of artificial intelligence increases with effort and particles.

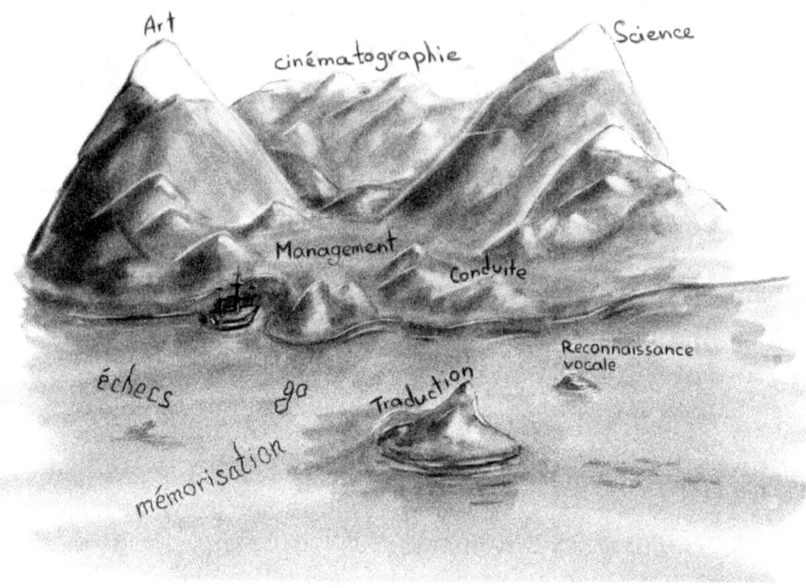

Figure 23: Reinterpretation of Hans Moravec's "Landscape of Human Skills".

The two challenges cannot be separated, because for many scientists, artificial intelligence and mass data can help solve part of the climate challenge. In 2009, the United Nations identified the value of big data for achieving the 17 sustainable development goals. The latter has initiated a wave of projects in this direction (e.g. the Global Pulse initiative, Pulse Labs). Thus, what might seem like a double collapse of the human species can lead to a form of symbiosis, a regeneration and could offer a way out. However, loss of control is possible and should be considered. Digital nature may well supplant human nature.

CHAPTER VIII

Possible extinction

Where artificial intelligence can destroy or save.

Will artificial intelligence achieve our hopes and bring solutions to the problems we face? Will it be sufficient and aware of our goals? Every being embarked on this journey, at this moment of time, of our history, of the great history, has no other choice than that of optimism, that of a saving technology, correcting our errors, repairing our tears, giving life to what seems lost by our actions. An artificial intelligence that saves man from himself. If we are right to be afraid, life has been battered regularly throughout its history. We have an obligation to dream and to hope. Nature is reborn, nature is adaptable, resilient. It optimizes its strengths, sustains species, ensures biodiversity, it calculates without counting. She knows how to die in order to be reborn, to remember and take back her rights. Life has had the time and the strength to survive many disasters. The proof is in the fossils. We read this difficult story by digging into the ground and back in time. The most famous, but not the most important of the extinction episodes, marked the end of the dinosaurs. Despite everything, none of these episodes would completely extinguish life, which never ceased to survive to relive better, even if it sometimes took more than a million years to recover. After five mass extinctions, should we fear a sixth episode of this type?

If man seems to be going beyond certain rules of nature, is he really doing so? Is moving forward always the best way to progress? Man has always advanced where nature has disappeared, on land, on seas, mountains and even underground and in the air. It may be our turn to step back in order to progress. If it does not seem reasonable to us to slow down a machinery that drives an entire system, then perhaps, yes, ultimately there will only be an artificial intelligence to remind us of our priority. Maybe it will know how to listen and find the right words to speak to men in the name of a silent nature. If artificial intelligence lent its voice and strength to nature, then our progress made sense. The two works would come together and could be reborn.

Great scientists believe that the future of humanity must go beyond the framework of this Earth which has borne us for so long, simply to avoid the inevitability of human disappearance. Maybe because this Earth is destroying itself, maybe because humanity is risking itself if it stays there. We imagine leaving and spreading to other planets. Artificial intelligence would then be seen as a point of hope. Demis Hassabis said: "I would be very pessimistic about the world if something like AI didn't come along the road. [...] If you look at the challenges society faces climate change, sustainability, mass inequalities - which are worsening - disease and healthcare, we are not making progress fast enough in any of these areas. Either we need an exponential improvement in human behavior - less selfishness, less short-term, more collaboration, more generosity - or we need an exponential improvement in technology. If you look at current geopolitics, I don't think we're going to get an exponential improvement in human behavior anytime soon. That's why we need a leap forward in technology like AI. "

Science has made us what we are today, beings not so far from reaching heights of understanding. Beings inferior in everything, but superior in everything to what has been in the past. In nature, in the universe, every particle carries with it some form of quantum information. Our world is thus turned upside down by an art whose common sense is losing us, and whose greatest experts agree on its incredible complexity. Quantum is however concrete, as concrete as a piece of paper or as any human being. These laws govern the infinitely small and offer us the most extraordinary experiences (e.g., Thomas Young's slits). If the quantum is a door to a New World, the quantum computer, and the biology which is not excluded from it, offer us a perspective.

DNA is undoubtedly a form of the software of life. It carries, on its scale, information. It is genetic. Unique information that is transmitted over time.

> As if what we are
> Every cell knew it.
> As if our identity was written,
> To the most anecdotal of men.
> As if to the tips of my fingers
> I knew who I was.

Man implemented solutions to conduct reverse engineering [103] while alive. We decode and understand it through the massive analysis of the genes of various species. A task which requires computer science, data analysis and genomics: time-lapse reading of the book of nature to understand more.

Our organic systems will imperceptibly become digital and information systems. Our information systems will imperceptibly become both organic and digital systems. The organic/digital duality, if it existed in our heads, is gradually fading.

CHAPTER I X
From organic to digital
From understanding a worm to controlling insects.

The Caenorhabditis Elegans is the first being whose genome has been completely sequenced. A very small transparent worm about a millimeter long. Like a leap forward, the Si elegans platform [104] presents the complete virtualization of the nematode and its environment. The ambition is majestic: to decipher and reconstruct the flow of information in the nervous system. A way to refine neural response models and link them to environmental interactions to reflect and understand biological reality better, and the biophysical events that lead to behavior. Understand with the head and the gesture this little transparent worm. A step before you offer yourself a bigger dream, immensely big. The software's features allow users to graphically create models of neural networks, and behavioral experiments on one of the most studied specimens in science. The simulation results can be obtained using a worm locomotion and a neural activity viewer.

A hybrid nature is emerging. Cyborg is the term which expresses with a word the convergence of cybernetics with the organic. A mixture of living and non-living taking shape and coming to life. We find a symbol of this trend with cyborg insects, insects controlled by humans with the help of electrical signals. Arthropods are equipped with electronic backpacks allowing them to be connected by WIFI (Figure 24). The researchers will have taken care to insert them with very thin electronic cables in certain regions of their legs or their wings. By sending microelectronic signals, by a nervous reflex, the animal stretches its legs and spreads its wings. In this system, the animal is controlled by a means that raises ethical questions.

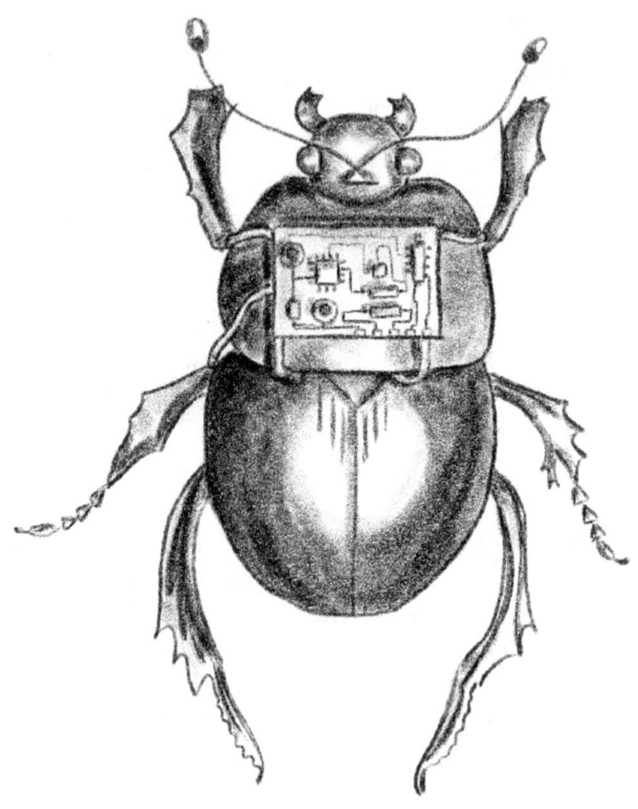

Figure 24: Example of a cyborg animal.

An insect that we manipulate with a remote-control console, as if to recall the dangerous game in which man has ventured, to warn of a possible direction for our own future. This project, already well advanced, is that of Hirotaka Sato, an aerospace engineer from Singapore. Its laudable purpose is that of making cyborg insects reach areas inaccessible to humans during rescue operations. These cyborgic insects could then sneak up to the rescue of humans in the rubble. The type of insects, their number, their timing should help overcome the limits of our drones. At this game, the flying insects outperform any man-made drone.

The pirouettes of our insects impress scientists, as do their low energy consumption. You have to observe them to realize that our imitations are certainly not as good. In this biomimetic game, inspiring, but lost in advance, science allows itself to save time, take a shortcut, by granting itself the authority to use living things. Is the aim to improve it or to make it a slave? This question is also transposed to the augmented man. We have in mind the image of an insect on its back, paws in the air. Each rises to the rhythm of the impulses sent by the electronic module. As the frequency increases, we understand the harm we are doing to the animal. Colonizing insects like this is sure to come at a price. The price of what is allowed or the permission to take everything.

The cyborg man is a possibility that, for some authors, has already materialized. Donna Haraway proposes in her manifesto a vision of the cyborg: "At the end of the XXth century, our time, a mythic time, we are all chimeras, theorized and fabricated hybrids of machine and organic; in short, we are cyborgs. This cyborg is our ontology; that gives us our policy. The cyborg is a condensed image of both imagination and material reality, the two joined centers structuring any possibility of historical transformation." [107]

A cyborg who understands himself as a being transformed by the machine and a machine transformed by man. Their fusion has already taken place through our interactions with technology. In the same vein, Katherine Hayles will speak of technogenesis to qualify the relationship between man and technology. This joint evolution leads man to modify his behavior through technology to the point of influencing what is most profound. The idea of the evolution of neural circuits is highlighted as a mark of technologies even in our flesh. A use that calls for a modification of the technique to satisfy new needs in a creation, and modification loop where the object becomes an agent. This observation would be doomed to materialize in an even more essential way with the new human-machine and brain-machine interfaces.

Is technology too serious a subject
to be left in the hands of thinkers?
Is technology too serious a subject
to be left in the hands of the leaders?
Isn't life too serious a subject
to be left in the hands of researchers?
Isn't life too serious a subject
to leave it in the hands of humans?

Jean Rostand predicted the paradox of power and life: "You kill a man, you are an assassin. We kill millions of men, we are a conqueror. We kill them all, we are a god." What will emerge from our laboratories? An assassin, a madman, a conqueror, a genius or a god? If all science begins as an art and ends as a philosophy, is it time to defend our schools of thought? We measure and sense the fragility of our planet. We feel our time is shorter. Stopping to admire the beauty that surrounds us would be almost an unconscious act. Just like putting words on a page to illustrate this situation. The urgency is topical and reminds us every day of our priorities. Everyone will find their own: consume, enjoy, marvel, worry, love, protect or wake up.

CHAPTER X
What future for our species?
Where the prophetic future is polarized.

I do not know whether to preach great upheavals to attract attention. In search of sensationalism or simply in a common sense conclusion, we read more and more prophecies which predict radical change, a new stage in our evolution, the consequence of an acceleration that we have difficulty in questioning.

Human jostle
Data is scrambling
Technology rocks us

Two prophecies that make the digital man two opposites at the same time. Proof that we can say everything and justify it, provided that we move far enough from the present in a skillful and aesthetic way. This freedom of words in our modern literature has led man into a doubt as crude as it is subtle. Am I a moron or a man-god? From a digital jerk [112] prefabricated to a *homo deus* with divine power, however great the man, however small he is, man is and will remain man. Nothing could be simpler and more banal.

He is the same man we see spending hours lining up crystals on a screen in search of varying rewards, the same man who hopes to see his luck smile by chance, the one who sometimes creates more of the work for others (?) than by his own efforts. The same. He acts for very meager rewards, bursts of color, virtual stones or candies, bits of land, more or less real fortune which will last for a while, not very long.

The man-god is the one we see beginning his road towards the mastery of life, towards the creation of synthetic and artificial life. The same that we have seen create a cell with a genome synthesized from scratch. A human hand has created life in a certain way. In an interview, the French political scientist Philippe Marlière went as far as to announce that we are at the dawn of the eighth day of creation.

With all his differences, all his colors and all his aberrations, his irrationality and his sensationalism, his creativity and all his hopes, I believe man is, and will remain, man. He is rich being what he is. Like the universe, he carries a story that has meaning. He is rich in what surrounds him, in what makes emotions without being sensational, rich in being able to marvel whatever his destiny, whatever his differences, his culture and his luck. We wouldn't trade anything for the stars, nothing against nature, nothing against nature. If the technologies don't set us back, then we will remain rich by this nature, rich by nature.

It is this nature that can teach us what our artificial intelligence has in store. She highlights forms of interaction between species that cover a range of possibilities. If an artificial life form could be understood as a new species, then nature's patterns are possible. The first takes place when species need to subsist to access the same resource present in limited quantities. In this scenario, they compete. Access to energy in different forms could play the role of this scarce resource and competition could arise. History could then find a winner or a balance.

The second pattern is that of exploitation. One species needs the other in order to survive. In the most critical case, it can be led to eliminate the other to ensure its survival. This is the prey-predator model.

It is possible that one exploits the other like a parasite. By means of this parasitization, one species survives and the other is then less endangered. Which man and machine will be the parasite? Isn't our technology already a form of parasite that lives at our expense? Man feeds the power of algorithms with this data.

Finally, in the less critical scenarios, a positive interaction is noticed. One species can benefit from the work of another for no consideration. This is the case for humans and bees - if we do not consider the recent impact that humans have on the disappearance of bees. An interaction can positively benefit both species. It can lead to a state of symbiosis where the two survive by the complementarity of the work of each other. This last scenario is the one we want. The one that allows us to continue our quest.

CHAPTER XI
A person-machine symbiosis
Where we hope for the best between man and machine.

If, for some thinkers, only man has a history, nature is nonetheless not devoid of language. It offers us stories within sight and within reach of those willing to hear them. American scientist Janine Benyus, a specialist in biomimicry, rightly reminds us that after 3.8 billion years of research and development, on a global scale, failures have become fossils, and what surrounds us contains the simple secret of survival. The fig tree and the Blastophaga psenes tell us a story: a natural and unfolded fable. This fable is a lesson in exchange, sacrifice, an ode to tolerance and sharing. Above all, it is a lesson in life.

The blastophagus and the fig tree

The happy fig tree produces profichi at the first light of spring
Inedible, they generate long-styled male flowers
As well as female flowers in short style
Style is important here because it protects from intrusion when it is long
The blastophagus, female insect rejoices in the situation
In a primordial sacrifice, she throws herself into the female flower lays there
and dies there

The larvae of both sexes then develop in their first shelter
They quickly become adults and fertilize
The cautious little male insects remain at the heart of the profichi
Intrepid females in kind, a first miracle occurs
As they leave, their bodies become covered with pollen from male flowers

Soon, the female has a new ambition
That of entering a summer fig
The latter are exclusively female and long in style.
This precious style prevents the insect from accessing it
In her failed attempt and by her body filled with pollen
She will contribute to life
But will not manage to parasitize the file
The latter will become edible by this natural process.

The cycle of life continues, and the mother figs arrive in the fall
In short style, interference is again possible
These mothers offer a winter shelter to these foreign guests
They will see a new day the following spring to continue the cycle
A cycle in search of profichi
Once again, the circle of life

What a remarkable story, teaches us nature
The fig tree provides a roof in exchange for survival
A roof that costs him two forgotten generations of fruit,
A dependence on common sacrifice
From an insect to a plant
One without the other, they are lost
Their symbiosis is essential

Like this fable, if the symbiosis is reached one day, a digital nature of man can emerge. We have two examples that offer an optimistic view of the future. A symbiotic phenomenon between man and machine has been highlighted by the Fold.it project. The latter allows humans to solve a problem that the machine cannot master on its own. It's about bringing in a host of players to solve puzzles to help understand a major biological process: protein folding. If we understand protein synthesis, how these form complex structures is still not understood.

The biologist François Jacob explained the surprising complexity of this task, which is still relevant today: "To general astonishment, a protein molecule, an architecture of rare complexity in three dimensions, is reduced to a structure of particular simplicity in one dimension. It is, in fact, a linear polymer formed by the end-to-end bond of a few hundred units taken from the assortment of twenty. The complexity in space arises from the folds of the chain on itself, from the sinuosities which hollow out a tormented relief on its surface: what gives the molecule its particular shape is the length of the chain, one hundred to a thousand units, and the sequence in which these units are arranged. Once again, diversity and complexity arise from the simplicity of a combination." [115]

We were able to create a symbiosis by delegating this task to humans to teach the machine. Via a form of 3D puzzle, the unfolding is offered to the players. Thanks to the techniques used, the machine can identify new ways of understanding the human approach. Cobotics is another picture of possible success between technology (the robot) and a man. Human-robot collaboration is thus conceived and executed, each making the best use of its capacities and complementing the weaknesses of the other. The robot is collaborative, it performs gestures with objects that are difficult for humans to achieve. On a production line, for example, he can grab parts that are too heavy, too small, or too hot. The human will complement him with acts that are difficult for the machine to perform.

The actions of man inspire the machine to accomplish tasks that it cannot do. The machine replaces the man on certain complex or dangerous tasks. How shall we conceive of our common future? Bio technologist and businessman Craig Venter said about the person-machine relationship: "My biggest fear is not the abuse of technology, but not using it at all and giving up. Losing a remarkable opportunity at a time when we overpopulate our planet and change environments forever. If we give up technology, we give up the means to use it to improve and save lives. The consequences of inaction can be more dangerous than the inappropriate use of technology." [116]

If we are uncertain about this becoming, we have however started large-scale work in order to fight against our destiny, to give us more time, to see a glimmer of eternity. Certainly, we have become aware of the possible directions of the digital nature of man. All the same, there remains a fundamental question: in the end, when will the end come, will death go away?

Section summary

Nature is a marvel, but also an endangered heritage. It offers us a comprehensible world which surprises us, which surpasses us and which we continue to discover. Technologies bring a new perspective on the lost beauties of our planet. In the midst of the thousands of lessons that nature can offer us, beauty, its mathematical order and the wisdom carried by trees are remarkable.

Faced with this nature, *homo sapiens* has unprecedented power. A power that allows him to change some of his rules and his environment. It has become Anthropocene. Tools have given man a stronger mastery of what surrounds him. Artificial intelligence seems to take over certain human functions to assist and replace him.

We are entitled to ask ourselves what the place of man in the face of artificial intelligence and nature will be. Our present observation, and that of a digital and organic nature that meet and whose borders are erased. Life science illustrates the situation: from a fully mastered worm to a cyborg insect. Man is now playing a dangerous game: the game of life. Will we reach a breaking point? What will be the place of man and artificial intelligence in this new nature?

We hope to achieve a form of symbiosis between man and machine, like nature offers us with the blastophagus and the fig tree. All dreams are allowed.

One of the highest stakes is still open, that of the fight against old age and the fight against death. The battle is on and that may be enough to frighten us. What would be the place of happiness in a world where the meaning of the act disappears, in a world where no one would feel more useful than an intelligent machine? What gratification and what goal to pursue?

When the end comes, death will go

Where man tries to fight against the effects of time and displays the ultimate goal of immortality.

"Immortality is a quest worth the wait"
Roey tzezana
"Hope to live long enough to live forever"
Ray Kurzweil

FIRST CHAPTER
The myth of Elizabeth
Where a woman wishes to fight against her fate.

We are in 2045. Elizabeth is getting ready to take the plane that will take her to Mexico to a biotechnology research laboratory working on a youth serum. The location of the center is kept totally secret - and for good reason - the experimental treatment which she wishes to undergo is not authorized by the American government. As a precaution, employees and customers will be kept anonymous.

Elizabeth is 44 years old, she has noticed for several years the harmful signs of time on her image, on her face. She refuses to admit defeat and intends to fight. To fight against this disease which creates wrinkles, which slows down her movements and which others accept too quickly under the simple name of old age. Refusing this fatality, she wants to extinguish and reverse the effects of age, the effects of time. She thinks about all the diseases that we have already managed to eliminate and she believes in the serum, she holds the remedy. Gene therapy is based on solid work and the first experiments promise (at least in mice) to restore the body to its former youth.

She has decided, she will take the plunge, even if the equation contains many unknowns. She takes an unmeasured risk. The impact of this treatment on humans has not been mastered and has never been tested. She will be the first. The first woman genetically modified to combat the effects of aging. She wants to take this risk to gain extra time, regain her youth.

In moments of fear and doubt, she keeps in mind these five lines of Louis Aragon, *Cantique à Elsa* [117] :

O my child, time is not for us
That a thousand and one nights are few for lovers
Thirteen is like a day and it's a flash in the pan
That burns at our feet, mesh for mesh
The magical carpet of our isolation
She is moved.

Love is the symbol of her dream
To love without farewell
She wants to put out this fire
This fire that burns in her
Out of her
This fire that burns its time
Time

CHAPTER II
The double treatment
Where his dream seems to come true.

Arriving at the center, the doctors take the first samples. They see the state of her cells. Those normally felt the first effects of her age. Treatment should reverse their condition. The first remedy is injected into her legs in order to block the myostatin which prevents the optimal growth of her muscles. The second aims to rejuvenate her aging cells. The doctor injects a gene necessary for the production of telomerase in several parts of her body. The enzyme's mission will be to enlarge the telomeres located at the ends of her chromosomes. As she knows, telomeric shortening is responsible for many diseases associated with aging. A Homeric discovery, our age and our lifestyle are responsible for this shortening. Nevertheless, artificially, it will lengthen them and wind up the hours and the hands of the clock.

The treatment proceeded very quickly. It is finished. Only time will tell if she was right. If it is reasonable to play with the effects of time, with your body, with life. Back home, she will have to wait a few months to know the result.

Time flies...

Six months later, the doctor sees Elizabeth again in her center for a first assessment. He takes a blood sample. The treatment does not seem to have generated any adverse effects. The patient is in good health and all of her physiological constants are normal. He then checks the size of her telomeres, her body clock. The wait is long, but his smile reassured Elizabeth - the treatment worked. The telomeres got bigger. Their lengths have been extended from 6.71 kilobases to 7.33 kilobases. She is now convinced of it, just like her cells, she feels rejuvenated... For the cells, this lengthening represents the equivalent of 20 years of human life. She thinks she was right to take the risk, at least for now.

CHAPTER III
When reality goes beyond fiction
Where 2045 becomes 2015 again.

This fiction did not take place in 2045, but really began in September 2015. Elisabeth is Elizabeth Parrish, the current president of BioViva [118] - a company specializing in biotechnology. This company has worked for many years on the development of treatments to reverse the effects of aging, making us live longer and healthier. Elisabeth had the two anti-aging treatments administered in her laboratory. She would a priori be the first woman to have undergone genetic manipulation to fight against the effects of age. Perhaps scientists know the cure for old age, she decided to test it in vivo on her own body. An intravenous injection of a gene necessary for the production of telomerase, the protein that stretches the telomere. She claims to be patient zero. Elizabeth Parrish is justified: "When I first became interested in this therapy, I considered it a crazy science. But we have to believe that the time for mad science has arrived."

For this, she and her employees relied on the discovery of telomeres and telomerase. Discovery that we owe to the remarkable team of Elizabeth H. Blackburn, Carol W. Greider and Jack W. Szostak. This breakthrough was recompensed by the Nobel Prize in medicine in 2009. This big step opened up new prospects for healing. However, the consequences of the treatment cannot be validated yet. Elizabeth's treatment was conducted without external controls of validity and without the required precautions. Obviously, in such a context, it is not reasonable. No more acceptable and conceivable than the possible impact of this new power conferred on men.

It is important to note that certain gene therapy treatments find their place in the fight against serious diseases. These treatments are subject to controls and have no comparison with this story, whose accuracy is uncertain. Can we then accept the use of this type of treatment in the case of so-called healthy patients? Under the simple effect of aging which one could, or not, consider as a disease? Changing nature and programming it as we wish may be acceptable in an ethical framework. In other cases, it appears to be an uncontrolled danger. The question is almost of a philosophical nature. What can we accept and under what conditions? Our ultimate goal is to push the boundaries of life. Is this wise?

Beyond aging, the subject of our ending is so sensitive that to put words on it seems almost indecent. Trying to win this fight is unfair, but winning it is even more unfair. We have all been struck by the predictable fatality of life that has caught us out of the blue. And we are hurt, hurt, comforted by our lost memories. Observing the financial energy with which man invests to get out of his infallible destiny, there again a feeling of indecency can take hold of us. If we fight to live longer, to attain immortality, or to erase diseases, it will never heal the wounds of those who could not be healed. Of those who didn't have the right treatment, got no cures, weren't born at the right time, just weren't so lucky. More simply, those who left quite naturally.

Should we conquer death so that the good merges with the true?
Would it be fair to fight against man's aging?
Or rather that there is just one man left?
To play with death is certainly more dangerous than to play with life.
Will man have the right to offer himself the rest of a lifetime once again?
To remain free in his mortal destiny.

A quest has already been launched in a direction that goes beyond all philosophy. If the fight against organic death seems futile in the short term, the fight against aging and its associated diseases carries a lot of hope. Results are noticeable. In their history, humans have benefited from technological advances on a regular basis. Artifacts are present on and in the body of humans in many forms. Some of these forms are very common, such as prostheses, but also rarer such as RFID chips implanted between the fingers of some humans. A pacemaker makes the man who carries it a man dependent on life or death according to an electrical impulse. The *quantified self* is a possible way for humans to monitor their health. Activity sensors monitor steps, others study your heart rate, blood, sleep, diet.

Retinal implants [122] allow blind people to regain part of their sight, relying on glasses that capture the environment through cameras. The images are processed by a minicomputer and are then transmitted by radio wave to a prosthesis integrated in the retina. The latter acts as a photoreceptor (cones and rods) to allow the patient to identify the contours of objects.

These latest advances identify the person who wears them in a unique way, allowing direct and permanent communication between the digital and physical world. The American giants have, in fact, started down this road towards the objective of an improved man, and even of the post-human.

CHAPTER IV
A giant's dream
Where the end is no longer the only thought.

Death is an almost constant thought for men. A species endowed with this consciousness. In his famous *Being and Time,* Martin Heidegger supports the importance of understanding the possibility of the impossibility of existence. He thus calls for a recognition of this consciousness. Behind this universal and persistent anguish of the unfinished, men have considered varied destinies. Will you have to travel in the solar barque of the god Re? Will you face judgment? Will you fall into nothingness? Will you join the light, the darkness? Will you leave in a new body envelope?
Epicurus seemed to have a rather detached view of death, to the point of proposing that death is nothing to us: an insistence on the need to seek happiness while distancing yourself from this fatality.

The giants of technology unashamedly display great ambitions: to pierce the barrier of death, or at least to make it tremble a little. Even if we accept that we do not know precisely what hides the other side of death. It is an eventuality that until now was prohibited to us by simple respect for our beliefs, respect for ancestors and by an obvious observation, accessible to everyone: none of the 108 billion humans who had the chance to live before us will have survived their fate, even though more than 6% of people born on Earth are still alive!

From now on, laboratories and research are in place to establish a treatment to fight back against aging. The French physician and anatomical-pathologist Marie François Xavier Bichat defined life as the set of functions that resist death. Thus, our ambition would be to push this life forward as far as possible to push back death. If we had abandoned this ambition when we understood that cell death could be programmed, would our current mastery of genetics allow us to rewrite this fate?

Men have decided to confront no longer it with spiritual weapons, but technological ones. Peter Thiel (co-founder of PayPal with Elon Musk), one of the dreamers of our destiny in *homo deus* and one of the greatest fortunes in the world would quote Shakespeare: "It is the common rule, everything that lives must die, carried away by nature in eternity". His response was "It may be true, but it is a truth that we must fight."

The GAFAMs (Google, Amazon, Facebook, Apple, Microsoft) have invested in projects of a sensitive nature to push back certain human limits. The stakes are exceptional and so are the investments. A fight against diseases, against aging or more simply a fight for immortality. Old age is perceived by transhumanists as a disease to be cured and not a fatality to be accepted. Jeff Bezos and Peter Thiel have invested in the company Unity Biotechnology whose goal is to reduce the effects of age and disease. Their subject of study is that of senescent cells (from the Latin *senex* - old man), which are cells at the end of their life. Work on mice has shown that removing such cells can have a positive effect on the animal's health. These cells have failed to divide through mitosis. As a rule, they secrete a substance which should allow them to be eliminated on demand. However, in some cases, the removal of this type of cells does not take place properly. They then accumulate and generate a large number of well-known pathologies with the effects of age.

Questions which seemed to belong uniquely to metaphysics and philosophy found a biological path. Genetics professor George Church says synthetic biology has the power to reinvent nature and reinvent ourselves. He says advances in biology could help extend human lifespans. He offers the following sentence: "I think we are very close. I think the world is at hand, as long as we don't have a setback."

When it comes to the fight against cancer, some robots no bigger than the thickness of a hair could help us. These organic nanomedicines are built on the basis of DNA origami. Two- or three- dimensional structures made from strands of virus DNA that may contain a healing substance. The latter is released thanks to a chemical gate which is activated on direct contact with the cells to be treated.

If curbing and stopping cancer is an important quest to extend life expectancy, Google has bigger ambitions. Larry Page announced a will to do more on this subject, recalling that the end of this disease would only save three years of our species' life expectancy: " You must think beyond. Think beyond what makes us mortals. Think beyond this privilege of death."

The methods of genetic modification are already there. Let us quote the genetic scissors CRISPR or more recently Prime editing. The discovery of the link between the level of NAD + and the prolongation of the lifespan in good health, but also of the whole lifespan. The implementation of NAD + precursor supplementation techniques with NR (Nicotinamide Riboside) and NMN (Nicotinamide Mono Nucleotide Nucleotide) molecules. These discoveries offer new perspectives. They make us think of our relationship to time in a different way. Far from being inevitable, regaining one's youth becomes partly possible on certain scales. The therapeutic opportunities are promising. The market associated with anti-aging treatments is only increasing. It was US $ 50.2 billion in 2018. Predictions indicate growth of nearly 6 % between 2018 and 2023. Professionals already offer products on the market.

We could very quickly grasp a new form of veracity in the relationship between money and time. Ethical considerations are, and should continue to be, part of the debate on the subject. This is still in its infancy.

If the quest for an eternal biological life is underway, can't digital technologies already offer us a semblance of immortality?

CHAPTER V
My last message
Where memory is a digital act.

On your digital journey, you might come across a blog whose last post has hundreds or even thousands of comments. Messages to remember, condolences, thoughts for the person who is no longer there while remaining visible through his works, his texts published online throughout a lifetime. Carried away by time, illness and sometimes by accident, the person is no longer, but continues to exist through his image, an image which now has a digital memory. It is possible to go back to your past and pretend to understand your life, wind up the clock on the list of messages to see it move backwards and forget fate for a moment. We review the photos, browse through the memories. We rediscover the words of a departed soul, as if his/her departure had once again colored the image of what she was. As if leaving, the traces of memory had given themselves a new dimension, a depth of incomparable beauty. We cling to small things, bits of a life that resonate with us. Snatches of memories which at the time they were flowing did not let us imagine their significance. Conversely, important moments in our lives are ultimately discreet in our heads. Our memory will not have sublimated them.

There are blog cemeteries, long lists of links to the abandoned pages of life. The questions of inheritance, rights and duties arises. Should we entrust our access to a loved one? Should we keep our writings online? Would you like to delegate your account or rather disappear forever from this digital image, disappear forever from both worlds?

Professionals are positioning themselves to support us in managing this digital future. Digital memorialist is a new profession. We also find wills, account management, life insurance and services for data transmission to trusted people. It is also possible to pre-program the sending of messages to certain members of your family. One agency says "this is a legacy you can give to your children and loved ones. You have learned several things about life from your experiences. Share your experience with your loved ones, inspire them by continuing to live through them."

QR-codes (two-dimensional barcode) have taken place even in our cemeteries. Symbol of the ultimate link that can exist between a life carried away and the digital data of an enduring story. A destiny carried in time, and which occupies in space no more than a small square. The code keeps a thread, a tiny link between the realms. A physical world, a digital world and a spiritual world that is written with belief.

The digital world could make humans survive with text analysis tools and sophisticated artificial intelligence algorithms. If we have been able to bring out new works by missing artists, can we use technology to simulate a life which has fallen, but which continues? We could hope, as with works of art, to see man reborn differently.

CHAPTER VI
A voice that defies time
Where a voice offers itself to eternity.

You have certainly already encountered this new form of software called 'dialogues' during your web browsing sessions. These *chatbots* are artificial entities capable of having a conversation with a human. Conversational agents, although often unconvincing, offer opportunities for interesting interactions. You will find them on websites or messaging applications. The famous paperclip with sympathetic eyes topped with eyebrows put on Windows in 1996/since 1996 may be one of your old memories. This curious character, named *Clippy,* accompanied you in writing letters on Microsoft Word. Far from this functional character, the adventure of James Vlahos is that of a man who will take the chatbot to a whole new dimension.

The American journalist has developed a unique and remarkable project thanks to technology. This journalist has always been passionate about chatbots. While his father John James Vlahos had to cope with disease, he wanted to keep the traces of his story and make it last. For this, he organized recorded discussion sessions, sessions where his father told his story, his passions, his experiences, facts about his family, how he met his mother, and so much more. Hours of recordings that could allow him to keep hold of the present memory of a destiny doomed to fly away. He spent hours and even days transcribing their exchanges on a machine. He wanted to give them a semblance of eternity.

His father faced the increasingly devastating effects of the disease and felt the fragility of his passage more and more. Hi son then had an idea, a crazy dream, to prepare a digital future for him. He focused his energy on creating a dialoguer. His *dadbot* or *robot dad* could transcribe his father's tone and humor, but also keep his anecdotes, his stories, his story. He could talk to it forever. Obtaining the agreement of his family, he set to work by exploiting all the recordings. Beginning with a simple way of greeting, or asking how he is doing, he continued his work to constantly improve his project. He continued the sessions with his father, until the day when his fate called him back and when, in reality, they parted. In his grief, he did not abandon his dream. On the contrary, he would make it an obsession. He explains his crazy ambition: "Even if it is only possible to have a very small chance of digital life after death, then the person I want to make immortal is my father." By dint of work, and after allowing his relatives to exchange with his *dadbot,* he adjusted his project to achieve a surprising realism. In 2017, he was invited to the Web Summit to present his creation, his crazy adventure, his digital father. A creation that aroused curiosity, concern, tenderness, and empathy.

Similarly to this project, audiovisual professionals have resuscitated the voices of John Fitzgerald Kennedy and even that of the Sun King. Voices that will encourage researchers to resuscitate others.

Making a voice survive is like dreaming of a form of immortality. Thomas Edison's invention in 1877 had already seemed to offer this dream. A sound which belonged to the unique present, then essentially to the past, was until then doomed to disappear. This same sound, its frequencies, its waves could now be recorded and could dream of another destiny. The voice could last and be transmitted to everyone whenever it suited them. The singer's timbre would no longer exist only in memory, but its author could over-exist. He could travel through time by the benefit of his voice. The phonograph offered a form of immortality. An immortality that is independent of the unique moment in the past when the voice landed in the machine, at the time of recording. When was that? Where was it? How old was he? What happened in the moments following the recording? Listening to a past that has become for a few moments our present, we forget the questions, and we immerse ourselves in the sound and the emotion. This moment that we live in the present is nevertheless an artistic residue of the past. We will have gone back in time beyond memory to something rawer, eternal. A crystal of time.

Like a vinyl turntable and the conversational robot, we understand the importance of data to create a computerized memory of our presence on Earth. This tool technology becomes memory technology. It undeniably retains something of us that is ascribable. If we are a material and spiritual being, then to what extent can the data we produce reflect who we are? Can we imagine having a digital twin that would survive us? A man in the matrix?

CHAPTER VII
The digital twin
Where we are digitized into a data twin.

Industry and the Internet have given rise to a new notion, that of the digital twin. It currently applies to objects and not to people. These representations are digital and dynamic simulations of the state of a real object. They are faithfully represented by computer according to the characteristics they present. Size, weight, shape, fragility, structure, materials, position, wear. To do this, the digital twins are modeled in real time and processed with the data captured. This approach combines computing power, artificial intelligence techniques and data analysis. It is used to manage the operation of ultra-connected devices such as the very next autonomous cars or certain aviation devices. These artificial models are faithful to their twin by adapting to their wear and their state of 'health'. Simulations and observations from the data make it possible to control the object, to project its behavior, but also to anticipate material fatigue, microcracks and optimize maintenance tasks.

It is likely that our society is in the process of obtaining its digital twin, a twin controlled and piloted by the giants of the web. These organizations do not hide their ambition, but already explicitly mention a 360-degree view of a customer or prospect. They deeply analyze what we are, in our texts, our images and our data. The same is true in e-health where patient monitoring can be done in real time and on many physiological parameters. The technology acts like a scanner developed to miss nothing and better cross-reference our data, ultimately to digitize it in the digital twin. Will we be faithfully represented according to our characteristic emotions, sensations, desires, ideas, originalities? This twin has the disturbing advantage of being realistic, mathematical, and comparable to billions of others. It allows a better understanding of its functioning, its specificity.

Should we fear that the fate of the twins will become entangled? Like our quantum particles that promise the future of the computer. What is at stake in the debate is whether one can influence the other, in this case a digital model on a real model. For entangled particles, the modification of one instantly causes the modification of the other, regardless of the distance between them. Let us hope that it will not be so with our lives. Our digital models would then make it possible to steer our behavior. Millions of digital marketing research articles confirm this hypothesis.

One thing is now confirmed: of the two twins, when one disappears, the other can claim to continue on his way. This vision of the digital twin could translate into a new surge of reality through person-machine interfaces, but also advances on subjects as imperceptible as consciousness. Man has developed machines from which we wish to emerge if not a form of consciousness, at least a modeling of the self, of their own existence. The idea of allowing a machine to conceptualize its being is a step in this direction. A representation that can enable perceptual, episodic and procedural learning (see the LIDA *Learning Intelligent Distribution Agent* framework). Researchers Bernard J. Baars and Stan Franklin argue that the functions of consciousness are produced by adaptive biological algorithms. Could machine consciousness be produced by similar algorithms?

This hypothesis is made all the more possible by imagining a technology capable of reading our brain waves or of simulating a brain on a computer.

CHAPTER VIII
A well-wired head
Where a mouse with a pierced skull becomes connected to a computer.

Will neuroscience and artificial intelligence soon be able to read our thoughts? Advances in brain-machine interfaces are promising, and regularly published studies show how much progress we are making in this area. The first objectives concern the restoration of motor and sensory functions and the treatment of neurological disorders. But with such technology, anything seems possible.

A study has shown the content of the possible by listening to our brain waves in order to reconstruct an image seen by a patient. This remains somewhat imprecise but gives a good idea of the starting image. The technique is sophisticated. A patient is seated in front of a projected image before him. Scientists measure his brain behavior with the help of functional magnetic resonance imaging. The latter makes it possible to visualize the brain waves in order to analyze them. The approach is made possible by measuring variations in blood flow and the magnetization of hemoglobin. A program will then adjust the pixels of the image to be reconstructed, to match the attributes of a deep artificial neural network with the attributes decoded from the brain imaging. To accomplish this task, the machine has access to a very large set of digital images. It uses a certain perception of the world. The authors summarize their contribution as a method of visual image reconstruction from the brain that can reveal both seen and imagined content by capitalizing on multiple levels of visual cortical representations. They specify: "We decoded brain activity into hierarchical visual characteristics of a deep neural network and optimized an image to make its characteristics similar to the decoded characteristics. Our method succeeded in producing images noticeably similar both to seen natural images and artificial images, while the decoder was only trained on an independent set of natural images. "

In another setting, in 2016, a paralyzed monkey was able to walk again thanks to a neurological device. The system is capable of listening to the commands relating to motor skills through an implant with a hundred electrodes directly located in the area of the brain that controls the legs of the primate. The data is transmitted wirelessly for analysis on a computer in real time. The latter decodes the movement intentions finally transmitting them to a stimulator located downstream of the injury and generating the movement. The final synchronization observed in the movement is almost perfect.

Brain waves start to speak to us through the computer. We hear them and wiretap them. Naivety or nature wanted us to ignore everything that is going on in a man's head apart from his actions and his words. Medicine and technology open a deeper perspective: respect for a private life which should not exceed the limits of the cranial box. Now, we pierce the skull of rats and listen to that of humans. There is no longer any need to write or speak to give substance to our ideas. They will be captured in their essence, at their genesis. We may not even realize it. Psychology and neuroscience come together. Psychology hardens, mathematics softens. Social neuroscience reflects this type of movement and changes in historical boundaries. The behaviors usually studied by social psychology are explored with a multidisciplinary perspective, finding an interaction between the functioning of biological and neurobiological systems and the phenomena of social psychology.

Figure 25: Image representing in vivo the connection of certain areas of the brain of a rat to a computer by a USB-C connection.

This is a step towards studying man according to the different scales and interactions between these scales, like the work that needs to be done for the analysis of the brain. Creative limits are pushed back. Pushed back by men who want to know and discover more.

Elon Musk is that type of man. The one who revolutionized online payment, then the automotive world with the electric Tesla, and who dreams of sustainable space transport with SpaceX. In July 2019, in his adventure towards the connection of man to machine, he presented for the first time the advances made by Neuralink. He then published an astonishing report presenting a rat with a brain connected via a USB-C interface (Figure 25). The objective of his presentation is, undisguisedly, to recruit talents to go further and faster. The company has developed a machine capable of inserting 192 electrodes per minute with exceptional precision. Each wire can be individually inserted into the brain with micron precision to bypass the surface vasculature and target specific regions. The electrode array is integrated into an implantable device containing custom chips for integrated amplification and digitization of low power signals. The 3,072-channel package occupies a size of less than 23 × 18.5 × 2 mm [3]. The photo is scary and intriguing. This image is only the first in a long series of human creations to come.

We cannot hear it without questioning our beliefs. If we hope to read a tiny part of the brain signals, we imagine one day downloading or uploading a new program to the animal. Using genetic engineering (or synthetic biology) is almost a given, but we can imagine the evil impact in the eyes of the ignorant. With a USB-C port on the head, everyone understands what's going on. The metaphor is different, but in either case, life will change, life will change. Understanding the human brain is obviously among the most ambitious projects.

The researchers identified brain activity related to motor skills from the study of certain populations of neurons located in the motor cortex. We would have succeeded in making a computer cursor move thanks to the measurement of the activity of neurons. In 2008, researchers at the University of Pittsburgh would take a new step forward by allowing the control of an artificial limb in real time. We then discover the surprising image of a monkey able to control an articulated arm in order to grab food to feed itself. The movement is carried out in three dimensions and the intake of food is ensured by brain activity only.

Other advances illustrate the progress made in the field of brain-to-brain interfaces (BBI). The interfaces of this type are capable of reading data from one brain and transmitted to another. In their most surprising demonstration, two researchers are connected not by thought, but by machine. On one hand, the brain activity is recorded with the help of an electroencephalogram, on the other hand, a transcranial magnetic stimulation makes it possible to transmit the instructions to the brain of the second researcher. In between, the data is digitized. While the first is practicing a game whose objective is to fire at the right time by simply thinking (no action), the other will be instructed to press the button to initiate the action. An example of cooperation between two brains whose demonstration is surprising.

Going further, the objective would be to create a network of brains that can work in collaboration. This vision is not utopian, since a first study has partially demonstrated its feasibility. Three people are involved in the experience of a Tetris game. Two members face the game and decide whether to rotate the block to be positioned. This information is combined between the two researchers, then transmitted to the last one who does not perceive the screen. The latter must, thanks to the data received, make the decision whether to carry out the rotation. The experiment allows a feedback loop to be performed by allowing both transmitters to evaluate the receiver's decision and re-send an order if the decision is not correct. Futurist Michio Kaku commented on this technology, indicating that brain networks will replace the internet. *BrainNet* will send memories, feelings, feelings on the internet.

The collaboration is not yet perfect, as it is unidirectional and based on binary judgment. Scientists remind us that this demonstration does not mean that we have understood how the brain works, let alone the thought mechanism. However, it suggests a possible future where our emotions, our memories are interconnected, a network of men and memories of men.

Let's continue our reflection to try to unravel the best kept secret in the world. Imagine how far man can fit into this digital nature.

CHAPTER IX
Digitize the brain, then the human
Where one seeks to unravel the best kept secret of our world.

The brain is at the heart of the issues, it allows us to perform the most surprising and unique tasks such as abstract thinking. Many projects focus on the digitization of the human brain, which many consider inaccessible, sometimes with reason, and not without the apprehension of discovering a biological and material reality hidden behind our first self or our invariable environment.

The brain is still largely unknown. However, like our progress in the observation of matter, our techniques have been refined with regard to the observation and capture of brain data. We have solutions more or less intrusive relying on magnetic and electrical signals. We are making progress on technologies that make it possible to capture and view brain activity in real time on human subjects. Magnetoencephalography, electroencephalography, electrocorticography and microelectrodes recording local field potentials are the main approaches used today. However, they cannot make us forget the complexity of the task. The brain is an organ that cannot be understood without considering its multiple scales of operation and the interactions between functional mechanics at different levels. The perspectives are varied and monopolize the stakes at different biological orders. Chemical, electrical and biological considerations must be taken into account at cellular, functional, atomic, molecular and organizational scales. While the way a simple neuron works is clear, neural networks are still poorly understood. To untie the threads of the intrigue, projects of exceptional magnitude have been carried out for many years.

One of these projects is the famous *Bluebrain* started in 2005 and later extended to the *Human Brain Project* (HBP). Its ambition is to offer a simulation, thanks to an in-depth analysis of the functioning of the brain. This detailed simulation must take into account the shapes of neurons, their electrical properties, including ion channels and other proteins. The task is extremely complex. The human brain has 300 billion cells. The neural network is made up of nearly 10^{14} synapses and more than 80 billion neurons. Everything is dynamic, neurons disappear, others are created, and synaptic connections evolve, just like chemical exchanges. The proposed simulations must approach the way the brain works by corroborating the measurements carried out on patients (captured with the methods already mentioned). Purely computational limitations are a major brake. If the regular increase in computing power makes it possible to progress, the most powerful supercomputers in the world cannot offer sufficient conditions to model at all levels a human brain in its unity, its entirety, and its complexity.

To unlock its secrets, brain activity should ideally be monitored and modeled in real time. However, the action potentials, which can be qualified as electrical information, do not last more than two milliseconds. Capturing, transcribing and simulating this level of complexity is one of the most important challenges of this century. To date, the HBP project has modeled the functioning of a small part of a rat's brain. The model can simulate 31,000 cells connected by 37 million synapses. To proceed, it will need 1.19 billion euros invested to allow a simulation of the human brain by 2024.

While the Grail is still a long way off, some studies have detected the neuronal signature of schizophrenia. Progress is also underway in the fight against Alzheimer's disease, but also in detecting the warning signals of a stroke or even repairing the lesions.

To understand the structure of the neural network better, and its importance in the different functions, there is a rather surprising approach: the culture. The aim is to develop a network of neurons on substrates in the laboratory. The culture of neurons is then carried out on grids making it possible to capture and send electrical activity to regular points. The culture of neurons on a substrate makes it possible to obtain a two-dimensional organic neural network whose connections are built in a few hours and whose spontaneous action is observed after a few days. This can be done from samples of rat hippocampal and cortex cells. In work dating from the beginning of the millennium, researchers at the California Institute of Technology have taken an astonishing step, that of the animate controlled by neural network. They control a virtual animal from the activity of a real neural network. The virtual mouse is placed in a simple room, allowing it the possibility of moving. The system then measures the action potentials on the neural network and transcribes them into the action of the mouse in the room. Encounters with virtual walls are reflected on the network. Ultimately, the analysis of the spatio-temporal patterns thus obtained could provide a better understanding of the learning mechanism. At this stage, the observations made by the researchers do not seem to provide usable data, but the effort is as remarkable as it is worrying. The concept of animation certainly needs to be put into perspective with a vision of the digital twin 2.0.

Finally, neuromorphic computing, imagined for more than 40 years, is inspired by the functioning of the brain in order to build new generations of computing chips that are more energy efficient and more efficient. Like the learning mechanism in the brain that results in synaptic plasticity, artificial chips are able to offer a form of plasticity. The work done to train this type of processor in the same way as humans has brought us an interesting lesson that echoes the beginning of this book. Computer scientist Yijing Watkins who is working on this issue says, "We are studying advanced neural networks, which are systems that learn like living brains do. We were fascinated by the prospect of training a neuromorphic processor in a way analogous to how humans and other biological systems learn from their environment during childhood development." [146] The approach used, however, posed many stability problems. Physicist and biologist Garrett Kenyon says, "The question of how to prevent learning systems from becoming unstable only really arises when you try to use biologically realistic and doped neuromorphic processors or when you try to understand the biology in it."

The solution finally found by the research team is surprising and yet very natural. They will expose the network to a form of Gaussian noise which seems necessary to acquire stability. A noise that researchers compare to that received by human neurons during sleep. This sleep, this exposure to noise would therefore be necessary to obtain stable operation. The researchers conclude with a phrase that resonates in the sense of the value of noise: "Slow wave sleep can work, in part, to ensure that cortical neurons do not hallucinate their target characteristics in pure noise, thus helping to maintain dynamic stability." Our biomimetic technologies must be inspired by noise and sleep to function properly. Our digital world seems to be building on the footsteps of our past discoveries. It opens new paths that resemble and remind us of our old nature.

With the progress observed, we thought that someday soon we would pass a brain interface. This will then be connected to the cloud. A possibility of freeing our mind by decentralizing certain tasks on remote computers. A way to free ourselves from our hands, our body, our limits and live in the clouds.

Russian entrepreneur and billionaire Dmitry Itskov dreams of immortality. To achieve his objective, he founded the 2045 initiative. This grouping works on the development of techniques whose ultimate objective is to achieve a form of immortality through avatars. The project is described as follows: "The first phase is to create a humanoid robot and a state-of-the-art brain-computer interface system. The next phase is to create a survival system for the human brain and connect it to the avatar. The final phase is to create an artificial brain into which to transfer the original individual consciousness." The progressive deadline is set at 2045 to allow an avatar to go through the four phases of its evolution.

Avatar A (2015-2020): A robotic copy of a human body controlled by a brain machine interface.

Avatar B (2020-2025): An avatar into which a human brain is transplanted at the end of its life.

Avatar C (2030-2035): An avatar with an artificial brain and whose personality is transferred at the end of a man's life.

Avatar D (2040-2045): A holographic avatar.

Will it be a future so free that there will be no body, no soul, no individuals, but only thoughts floating in a 'cyber soup', like a return to the primordial soup, the same one as the world's? The origin of life? Will we be entitled to this moment of regeneration or to spirits blocked forever? Anticipating risks, taking them seriously and using our intelligence should allow us to progress, to protect ourselves and to control the situation, in order to keep our place as a man who thinks. As Oscar Wilde said, men who even from the gutter can gaze up at the stars without losing their minds [148].

CHAPTER X
Let's not forget the humanoids
Where robots enter the future.

Plato's famous quote on death questions us: "Is this something other than the separation of the soul from the body?" We die when the body, separated from the soul, remains alone, apart, with itself, and when the soul, separated from the body, remains alone, apart, with itself. If the soul is immaterial and immortal, how can we synthesize it or even give it material support? Does it take place in our brain or is it disconnected from it? According to Isaac Newton, it is the spirit that is born in the brain.

Far below the question of the soul, that of a conscious and general artificial intelligence is open. The contribution of Sophia, the humanoid robot created by David Hanson could be of great help. The robot with Saudi nationality can recognize the movements, gestures, and emotions of men. She shares their words and even offers television interviews. Born in 2015, she can simulate communication with men in a convincing and efficient way. She is also able to draw a person's face freehand.

By producing this anthropomorphic robot in hundreds, then in thousands, of copies, by marketing it on a large scale, it could be useful for our daily tasks. Robots of this type are connected to a single artificial intelligence that takes place in cloud computing. By imagining the popularization of Sophia and her presence in homes, human behavior could be observed and uploaded to the cloud in real time from many points in space. All the robots would instantly learn from all our behavior. Each Sophia would become a source of information, which would allow it to better understand our behavior and gradually enrich the level of its intelligence. This mass effect could help bring us closer to the ultimate goal. The sequel has been envisioned in many works of science fiction.

Professor and great writer Isaac Asimov had a critical eye of science fiction offering a dystopian and simplistic view leading to machine control over humanity. He indicated in the preface to volume 1 of the *cycle of robots*: "If robots are so perfected that they can imitate the process of human thought, it is because the nature of this process will have been designed by very smart human engineers. They will have incorporated safety devices." It is precisely in this context that he invented the famous laws of robotics. He envisaged a logical, ethical framework that man would have fixed and integrated into the machine.

Law 1: A robot cannot harm a human being or by remaining passive allow a human being to be exposed to danger.

Law 2: A robot must obey orders given to it by a human being, unless such orders conflict with the First Law.

Law 3: A robot must protect its existence as long as this protection does not conflict with the first or second law.

Whether or not our future is made up of thinking machines, with regular progress the question of the safety of our machines remains omnipresent. It is measured by Moore's Law (Gordon Moore) or the Law of Accelerated Return (Raymond Kurzweil). Two laws that remind us that our power is not only growing, but even seems to be accelerating in recent years.

Asimov's three laws were adapted as part of a robot ethics charter project in South Korea. An example of a fictional work that once again takes shape in our reality. If some robots are gradually approaching man, man has also improved to offer an extension of possibilities.

CHAPTER XI
Humanity 2.0 or Life 3.0?
Where man would enter a new phase in his history.

Transhumanism is not not simply a theoretical movement, it also results in practices aimed at strengthening the intellectual, physical and psychological capacities of humans. Robocop, Avatar, Terminator or more simply Elizabeth Parrish, the patient zero of BioViva are strong images for us. The international non-governmental organization, Humanity +, campaigns for the ethical exploitation of new technologies within the framework of transhumanism.

Drugs that alter mood, substances that promote mass gain, selective erasure of memory, are all examples that illustrate how technological advances are already about to improve humans and alleviate its condition. Some substances belonging to the nootropic categories are mentioned because of their effects on the cognitive abilities of man. The use of drugs to improve one's state of well-being without having a real therapeutic need was highlighted by the psychiatrist Peter Kramer in his book *Listening to Prozac*. He defines this practice as cosmetic pharmacology. He specifies that some humans may seek a higher state of natural well-being, with the use of antidepressants. An ethical debate about the taking of these substances by healthy patients for the simple purpose of improving a state of well-being is underlined. The same question arises for all substances that can be used to improve the performance of memory, creativity, attention or motivation.

American futurist Ray Kurzweil, employed by Google in 2012 as technical director, describes in a report his vision of the human in version 2.0. He predicts a convergence of non-biological intelligence with our biological brains for 2030. He believes that our intellectual and physical capacity will then be considerably improved.

In the same vein, Max Tegmark, the Swedish cosmologist from MIT presents a look at the evolution of life, in his book, *Life 3.0 Human Being in the Age of Artificial Intelligence*. He describes three successive versions. Version 1.0 is organic. It lies in the ability to survive and reproduce without being able to change or adapt in real time. It will take a very slow cycle of evolution to move from this first form of life to the next. In its version 2.0, life has acquired the possibility of improving itself by modifying its software through knowledge, language and learning. Finally, the last form is capable of making its software evolve, but also its body, its organs: its material support. It could change its envelope in an accelerated manner without resorting to Darwinian evolution. This 3.0 form appears credible today, because matter is programmed and can become intelligent.

Is the fate of humanity solely in the hands of men? Is it conceivable to consider a future of man as a *homo deus,* a man-god who will not know how to save himself from himself? Shall we view Life Form 3.0 as a human form or a hybrid? If we keep asking questions about the robot laws, what are the rights of enhanced /improved men?

While he is waiting to see whether such a form of life is certain to arrive or not, Raymond Kurzweil projects himself into his imaginary future where everything seems possible.

CHAPTER XII

If he survives Ray?
Where a man might wake up in the future.

In this quest for immortality, as a last resort, Raymon Kurzweil has put his confidence in the Alcor life extension foundation. Immediately after his biological death, he will be taken care of by this company specializing in cryonics, vitrified in liquid nitrogen while maintaining, as much as possible, the state of his cells thanks to cryoprotectants. This being is no longer just on his way to death but is convinced that he can survive it. He is one of the few men going into the unknown. He doesn't know if the future will enable him to wake up or if he won't. He has therefore offered himself a lottery ticket to a new life – will it be a winner?

How can we know if science will be enough to bring this body back to life? When? And under what conditions? A remarkable humility. If future generations opened the door of life to him again, this brilliant spirit of our century could quickly appear as under evolved when he wakes up.

What will he be able to see?
What will remain of our Earth?
Of our forests, our arts, and our species?
Vestiges of another time
Kingdoms from another era
A man is possible.
A man to see what the past was.

This man hopes to wake up someday in the future. He will be able to relate, like a resurrected pharaoh, the stories of a distant past, which is, and will remain when all is said and done, a banal present. A present retraced by an out of phase futurist.

In the midst of our history, this uncertainty, nature again appears to have exceeded fiction. We will therefore end our overview with a funny fairy with naturally magical power.

CHAPTER XIII
A case goes beyond the paradox
Where to close his path, the author points the paradox of time upside down.

Is it possible to live forever or re-emerge from our old age? Biological reality provides answers that go beyond our common sense. Without tapping into philosophy or technology, the observation of life continues to surprise. We have crossed plant species with the power to freeze and, if not to stop time, to stop their metabolism. In simple ignorance we observe with pleasure the Rose of Jericho without really worrying about understanding its secret. Selaginella lepidophylla, native to the Chihuahua desert, has developed extraordinary faculties necessary for its survival. This parched ball can come back to life on contact with water. It withstands several years of drought, weighing no more than 3 % of its usual mass. It freezes in a state of cryptobiosis and can wait months and years before waking up. Extremophile organisms sometimes seem to deviate from the principles that are essential to life. Is this a message of the path we must follow? Could there be a hidden message?

A Hindu legend prompts reflection. It relates a time when all men were gods. Abusing his power, as is often the custom, the creator-demiurge god of Hinduism Brahmā makes the decision to withdraw this supreme gift from men. He plans to hide it to make it inaccessible. An exchange takes place to define a safe place to put the treasure.

The discussion begins as follows:

- Let's bury the divinity of man in the earth (*our history?*).
But Brahmā replied:
- No, that is not enough, because the man will dig and find it.
Then the gods replied:
- In this case, let's throw the divinity in the deepest oceans (*life?*).
But Brahmā replied again:

- No, because sooner or later man will explore the depths of all oceans, and it is certain that one day he will find it and bring it to the surface.

Then the minor gods concluded:

- We do not know where to hide it, because there does not seem to exist on earth or in the sea of a place that man cannot one day reach.

So Brahmā said:

- This is what we will do with the divinity of man: we will hide it deep within himself, because it is the only place where he will never think of seeking (*consciousness?*).

Homo sapiens dug the earth. He discovered that the earth had a history. She even carried vestiges of her own history through fossils. He explored the bottom of the oceans. He discovered that life was certainly born there. He opened his skull, deep inside himself, what will he discover? He seems to have found this place but has yet to uncover all its secrets.

Nature, life, myths provide puzzling examples. Could man control time as he has successfully learned to do with matter, other men, life and a tiny part of space? He has the power to change his environment, to make an impact on it. Even if the act is not glorious, it is for the first time able to change a complex and specific mechanism. He will have succeeded in piercing the ozone layer and thus piercing part of his destiny. His actions make time evolve and speed up our history. Progress is accelerating. Progress that gives us the hope of living. Man's actions could ultimately change our fate. What can man do in this time that is flowing and slipping through his hands? Can he slow it down? It seems to exist outside of everything and to be the origin of everything. His actions are inscribed and lost in time.

Stephen Hawking had not completely abandoned the theoretical possibility of time travel. After all, we are all constantly traveling through this time. This trip has given us life. It is true that we are bathing in this shifting present. A journey that counts every second, every minute, every hour and every day. We celebrate first names, birthdays and stories of great men. We choose everything about this trip but the moment to enter it, to leave it and the meaning of it. Space leaves us free; time imposes its direction. If time loops offer clues to going back in time, they do not seem to accomplish their mission satisfactorily. We will bathe in an old time from a very different new one. Going up our path then seems to contradict our ambition. There is no hope left for man to change this impalpable destiny of the future.

Finally, we will have to defer to the physicist and philosopher Étienne Klein who suggests not confusing the reversibility of time with the reversibility of physical processes. We will merely make some reversible processes. Make the skin younger, lengthen our telomeres.

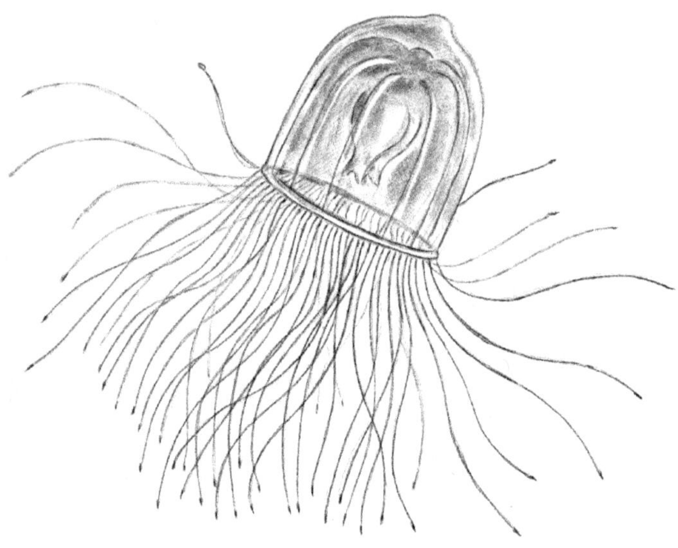

Figure 26: Turritopsis nutricula is a jellyfish of the hydrozoan class that does not measure more than 4 to 5 millimeters.

A small being has pushed the vice to the maximum. He can go back through his youth several times. If scientists, poets and artists imagined it, Turritopsis nutricula did it (Figure 26).

CHAPTER XIV
Turritopsis nutricula the fairy
Where a jellyfish has its head upside down.

Life sometimes goes beyond the paradox of time
A unique jellyfish has this natural talent
This hydrozoan holds the power
It becomes a young polyp again
It turns back the clock
It is an unusual metazoan
Whose cycle of life still turns
Turritopsis nutricula may still rejuvenate
Holding the secret of biological immortality
It only dies in a sort of Cornelian tragedy
Looking ahead, it goes back in time
In the face of danger, it goes back in time
It doesn't know what it's doing here
But the paradox of time
It knows!

Not all Men have sought to become eternal or immortal. Most made the happiest and most reasonable choice, they just lived. Through the course of history, many cultures and characters have embarked on an impossible quest akin to a form of immortality. It is this strength to want to outlive life that has allowed the realization of remarkable buildings. It is the work of many artists, politicians and scientists to want to go beyond the limits, to escape from the 'rules of the game', yet those which teach us to live. If thinking about death is a way of learning to live, Montaigne teaches us that to philosophize is to learn to die. By trying to go beyond the limits offered to him, man transcends himself in art and science. He surpasses himself in time and space. He offers himself unattainable journeys with boats, cars, rafts, trains, rockets or words, thoughts, art, digital, *likes* and selfies.

He offers himself a memory which, beyond his own, allows him to subsist furtively in that of others. It is perhaps by trying to go beyond our limits once again that we will discover or create a remarkable edifice. If the goal is not achieved, new lessons may still be learnt. Those offered by nature, by our knowledge and by the richness of our intelligence. Decidedly, the great book of nature is not about to close.

Section summary

212

Science and technology give us new power to fight our destiny. The Elizabeth myth has shown us to what extent biological engineering can reverse the effects of time, the effects of age. Between reality and fiction, however, we do not know where to position the future of man. The dream of the giants is to roll back or even wipe out old age. They invest in this chimera which offers signs both of hope and fear.

We can imagine surviving the effects of our death for a short time. Leave messages to say goodbye beyond the afterlife. Voices rise in time as if to keep an imprint in the reality that has disappeared from us and the interfaces between technology and the brain are underway.

Will we be able to digitize the brain or more simply to synthesize it, to duplicate it? Will we be able to build digital twins, artificial clones? The situation raises many ethical, moral, and philosophical questions.

What will happen to the future of man and his humanity: will he be a hero of his life, or a hero of his death? What will become of a general artificial intelligence capable of surpassing us? To believe in this immortality at this precise moment in humanity when we are in doubt, some have chosen cryogenics. This choice is a hope, but also a belief in a future reality.

Nature has taught us that some effects of time are reversible. However, she did not teach us what philosophy will be necessary to maintain happiness under these conditions.

With or without immortality, time can feel like sips of dry water. With or without immortality, every drop of time can give you the scent of paradise.

Conclusion

For millennia, man has sought to understand nature, the universe, to exploit his faculty of creation and reflection. He has never ceased to design ever more efficient tools and sciences. The message offered to him in nature could lead us to believe that he has discovered her secret and his dangerous share of responsibility. A responsibility that goes beyond him. His genius, his creativity, his beliefs have recently opened the doors to what he is. Deep down? Beyond or below its expectations, neurosciences, biology, technology offer a possible mechanical, digital, chemical secret of man above men.

The boundaries apparently separating science, art, philosophy, reality and its representation have gradually been erased. Leonardo da Vinci saw the existence of the object without conceiving of its limits. He said with genius: "The outer limits of the object do not belong to the object at all, for the end of one thing is the beginning of another." Limits occupy no place. Like *sfumato,* it is difficult to define the limits of the man of tomorrow, of the post-human. Today's surprised us so much.

We have read the essential bricks of life and the processes of creation, division, reproduction. If we have not yet found the secret of the gods, we have indeed created life artificially, without inheritance. A power that has even made it possible to revive an extinct species. Far from science fiction, in our laboratories, the improbable has indeed already taken place. The Pyrenean ibex disappeared in 1999, at the same time as the last representative of its species called Célia. Man would rewrite her tragic destiny in 2009 after years of trying. A clone was born thanks to tissues taken at the time. The task turned out to be remarkably complex. Out of several hundred embryos, one single clone was born. An extinct species was reborn. Man no longer wrote his own story and his destiny, but rewrote that of an extinct subspecies. Historic and unique minutes, before this clone was called to death by a lung defect. A reminder of the dangerous game we have become attached to.

While going back in time still seems inaccessible, tracing our mistakes is possible. Despite all the poetry in the world, it seems all the same forbidden to be stopped at this hour on the face of the watch.

However, by dint of healing everything, it is possible that our fragility could pass and disappear. If an immortal man is announced one day, what will become of our previous statements. At an eternal hour, taking care of yourself becomes ridiculous. Time disappears, and here it is again in the unknown, in eternity. In the absence of fragility do not catch cold would not make sense. Will we not lose our strength and our sense? Does "I love you" have a weight in immortality? Millennia of stories of our cursed couples have counted this romantic, romantic epic. The eternal love of Tristan and Isolde, of Paul and Virginia, but also of Orpheus and Eurydice, are just a few examples among so many others whose fate is miraculously written every day. Louis Aragon told us that there will always be a quivering couple for whom this morning will be the first dawn. During a lifetime, love is consumed and weakened. It takes on its full meaning in eternity, separated by death. It becomes untouchable and memorable.

At the end of this journey, a little dazed, back on Earth, back home, I observe the familiar landscape of my garden. The one whose contours surrounded my childhood. I find the same shapes, the same basin, the same trees and a blooming nature. A nature that has evolved peacefully, in almost silent secrecy. Far from the hustle and bustle of my life, far from the hustle and bustle of our lives and far from my eyes. After such a journey through the technological world and so many seemingly supernatural discoveries, I almost feel uncomfortable facing the garden again. In our last decades, so much ground has been covered and on so many subjects. We perceive the beginnings of the digital nature of man. This nature, usually so adaptable, does not seem to be aware of what is going on. What is she planning? Could she anticipate the almost inordinate power that is about to enter human hands? Natural selection seems so slow and so little in the face of a man running frantically. Faced with this, I feel her fragility, from another time, from another era. I too already feel from another time, from another era. Listening to the birds singing, I worry about this piece of garden. Could this haven of peace afford a form of eternal life? Will it be saved or destroyed by the tools of man? Beyond keeping it in my memories, I would love to believe that this piece of Earth, like so many others will be saved by a miracle equal to the one that made them possible. I would like to think that knowledge is not (just) a weapon, and that technology is not harmful. And yet I doubt. I have this concern. I'm afraid for this little corner of the garden from my childhood.

If in the eyes of men, nature may seem cruel, in the eyes of nature, man is too. In this discussion, we have kept the beauty of nature and the cruelty of man. The opposite choice would have been possible. However, it could not have been the opportunity to put *homo sapiens* face to face with his fate. Let us keep those responsibilities firmly in our hands. Let us do our trial as a responsible man and not as an animal: to sublimate oneself, without falling into pitfalls of possession, power, and control. Let us elevate ourselves the better to find our anecdotal place in nature and the universe. We can no more naturally denature humanity than humanly denature nature.

Faced with these concerns, these possibilities, and to offer us a way out, we need philosophy more than ever. If genetic engineering has already precipitated this imperative (for example Jacques Monod in 1973), artificial intelligence, synthetic biology makes it even more urgent and concrete. It is perhaps philosophy which will be the ultimate essential to advance our machines, to code our morality. A philosophy linked to a digital humanism.

If man has never ceased to think about man and more recently the machine, he must now think about the machine in his humanity.

Table of content

Bibliography

[1] Adrien Jaulmes, Gregory F. Treverton, The world in 2035 as seen by the CIA and the National Intelligence Council: the paradox of progress, 2018.
[2] Charles Perez, Digital Prison, Contemporary Questions, L'Harmattan, 2020.
[3] Google CEO Sundar Pichai compares impact of AI to electricity and fire, Lauren Goode, The Verge, January, 2018.
https://www.theverge.com/2018/1/19/16911354/google-ceo-sundar-pichai-ai-artificial-intelligence-fire-electricity-jobs-cancer
[4] Mythology tells us that the theft of fire is not the only reason for the torment of Prometheus.
[5] Milad Doueihi, For a digital humanism, Seuil, 2011.
[6] McLuhan Marshall. Understanding Media: The Extensions of Man. 2nd edition. Abingdon: Routledge, 2005 (first published 1964).
[7] Nancy Katherine Hayles, Ho w We Became Posthuman: Virtual Bodies in Cybernetics, Literature, and Informatics, 1999.
[8] Cynthia Stokes Brown, The Meaning of Big History, Philosophically Speaking, Dominican University of California, 2016.
[9] Daniel Kahneman, System 1 / System 2: The two speeds of thought, 2011.
[10] C. Vallaux, Mists and aerial dust in the area of the Cape Verde Islands, Annales de géographie, 1930.
[11] Ross Donaldson, Gerald Buller, and Alessandro Fedrizzi Satellite-based quantum communications (Conference Presentation), Proc. SPIE 11134, Quantum Communications and Quantum Imaging XVII, 2019.
[12] William Dalrymple, The Singer of Epics in Nine Lives, Bloomsbury, 2009.
[13] K. Gödel, Über formal unentscheidbare Sätze der Principia Mathematica und verwandter Systeme, I. (" On formally undecidable propositions of Principia Mathematica and related systems ") Monatshefte für Mathematik und Physik, 38, p. 173-198. Translated into English by van Heijenoort in From Frege to Gödel. Harvard University Press, 1971.
[14] Adrienne Mayor, Bio-techne, Half-human soldiers, robot servants and eagle drones - the Greeks got there first. Could an AI learn from their stories?, 2016.
[15] Michelis, Enrico. El problema de las ciencias históricas / Enrico de Michelis. Serbiula (sistema Librum 2.0), 2020.
[16] Étienne Klein, Conversations with the Sphinx, Albin Michel, 1991.

[17] Jordan, SF, Rammu, H., Zheludev, IN et al. Promotion of protocell self-assembly from mixed amphiphiles at the origin of life. Nat Ecol Evol 3, 1705–1714, 2019.

[18] Mark Strauss, Twelve Theories on Human Evolution, and Why They're Wrong, Killers? Pickers? Craftsmen? Scientists find it difficult to agree on the essence of humanity and its origins. https://www.nationalgeographic.fr/evolution/douze-theories-sur-levolution-humaine-et-pourquoi-elles-sont-fausses, 2019.

[19] Hesiod, Theogony, VIII [th] century BC. J.-C.

[20] Brigitte van Wymeersch, Pythagorean philosophy of numbers and music, in 1997.

[21] Boèce, De Institutione Musica, foundation of theoretical musical speculation of the Middle Ages, c. 470-525.

[22] The encyclopedia is largely available online. https://gallica.bnf.fr/conseils/content/lencyclopédie-de-diderot-et-d'alembert

[23] This was a scientific hypothesis which stipulated that water retained an imprint of substances with which it had been in contact (My truth on the "Mémoire de l'eau" by Jacques Benveniste, Au cœur de l'extra-ordinary, Henri Broch). The original article was published in Nature Human basophil degranulation triggered by very dilute antiserum against IgE, Nature vol. 333, June, p. 816, 1988.

[24] Jacques Monod, Chance and Necessity. Essay on the Natural Philosophy of Modern Biology, Seuil, 1970.

[25] Mnih, V., Kavukcuoglu, K., Silver, D. et al. Human-level control through deep reinforcement learning. Nature 518, 529–533, 2015.

[26] Daniel Geng and Rishi Veerapaneni, Tricking Neural Networks: Create your own Adversarial Examples, 2018.

[27] A. Bonnet, AR Grosso, A. Elkaoutari, E. Coleno, A. Presle, SC Sridhara, G. Janbon, V. Géli, SF de Almeida & B. Palancade, Introns protect eukaryotic genomes from transcription-associated genetic instability. Molecular Cell, 2017.

[28] Pyrrhon or appearance, puf, Marcel Conche, 1994.

[29] According to the title of Henri Hatlan, 1979.

[30] Henri Bergson, La Pensée et le Mouvant, Paris, 1934.

[31] Roman Jakobson, Essays in General Linguistics: The Foundations of Language, 1963.

[32] Article 528, Amended by Law n ° 99-5 of January 6, 1999 - art. 25 JORF January 7, 1999 " Animals and bodies are movable by their nature which can be transported from one place to another, either because they move by themselves, or because they can only change place by the effect of a foreign force ", 1999.

[33] Frei Henri. The Grammar of Faults, 1931.

[34] William Labov. Principles of linguistic change: Social factors. In the series, Language in Society 29. Malden, MA: Blackwell Publishers, Inc. 2001.

[35] André Comte-Sponville, Dictionnaire philosophique, puf, 2001.

[36] R. Alexander Bentley, The Acceleration of Cultural Change: From Ancestors to Algorithms (Simplicity: Design, Technology, Business, Life), 2017.

[37] Diana Walsh Pasulka, The Prehistory of the Posthuman, 2017.

[38] M. Ben Hamed and P. Darlu, Genes and Languages: a long common history? The Bulletins and Memoirs of the Anthropological Society of Paris, 2008.

[39] Carl Sagan, Pale Blue Dot: A Vision of the Human Future in Space, Random House, New York (ISBN 978-0-679-43841-0), 1994.

[40] Frank D. Drake Is anyone out there? the scientific search for extraterrestrial intelligence, Delta Book / Dell Pub, 1994.

[41] Isaac Newton, De mundi systemate, 1728.

[42] Adapted from page The Golden Record Cover, https://voyager.jpl.nasa.gov/golden-record/golden-record-cover/

[43] https://www.archmission.org/

[44] Catling, DC, Krissansen-Totton, J., Kiang, NY, Crisp, D., Robinson, TD, DasSarma, S., et al.. Exoplanet Biosignatures: A Framework for Their Assessment. Astrobiology, 18 (6), 709–738, 2018.

[45] Rachel Feltman, " Stephen Hawking annonce $ 100 million hunt for alien life ", Washington Post, July 20, 2015.

[46] Molecular Biology Reports, Volume 45, Issue 5, pp 1479–1490, Trends to store digital data in DNA: an overview, 2018.

[47] Shipman SL, Nivala J, Macklis JD, Church GM. CRISPR-Cas encoding of a digital movie into the genomes of a population of living bacteria. Nature, July 12, 2017.

[48] A video with further explanations can be viewed at the link below. Movie Replayed From Living Cells' DNA Debuts Molecular Recorder, https://www.youtube.com/watch?v=gK3dcjBaJyo

[49] Kalff, F., Rebergen, M., Fahrenfort, E. et al. A kilobyte rewritable atomic memory. Nature Nanotech 11, 926–929, 2016.

[50] Stephen Hawking, Brief Answers to the Big Questions, Hodder & Stoughton, 2018.

[51] Khalil Gibran (1883-1931), author of The Prophet.

[52] The Plank wall is described as the moment from which our standard models no longer allow us to know the above.

[53] Jean d'Ormesson, Almost nothing on almost everything, Gallimard, 1995.

[54] Jean D'Ormesson, One day I will go away without having said everything, Robert Laffont, 2013.

[55] Guido d'Arezzo, Micrologus, 1026.

[56] Leonard d e Vinci, Thoughts on Art and Life, 1906.

[57] If many algorithms use similarity measures, segmentation algorithms aim to create homogeneous groups, multidimensional boxes.

[58] Urban Watercolor Sketching: A Guide to Drawing, Painting, and Storytelling in Color, Book by Felix Scheinberger, 2011.

[59] Creativity has been identified by the World Economic Forum as one of the most promising skills. Conversely, a third of today's skills will no longer make sense in five years. WEF, Riad, 2017.

[60] Mayor, Adrienne. Bio-techne: Half-Human Soldiers, Robot Servants, and Eagle Drones — the Greeks Got There First. Could an AI Learn from Their Stories? " Aeon, May 16, 2016. https://aeon.co/essays/replicants-and-robots-what -can-the-ancient-greeks-teach-us.

[61] Eduardo Kac, "Move 36", 2004,   http://www.ekac.org/move36.html

[62] Emery Schubert, Sergio Canazza, Giovanni De Poli & Antonio Rodà, Algorithms can Mimic Human Piano
Performance: The Deep Blues of Musi c, Pages 175-186, 2017.

[63] https://www.ibm.com/watson/services/personality-insights/

[64] https://obvious-art.com

[65] http://deepdreamgenerator.com

[66] Adrienne LaFrance, When Robots Hallucinate, What do Google's trippy neural network-generated images tell us about the human mind?, September 3, 2015.

[67] Stephen Hawking, A Brief History of Time. From Big Bang to Black Holes, 1988.

[68] Marcus Vitruvius Pollio, On the subject of architecture, architectural treatise, 1st century BC. J.-C.

[69] https://www.nextrembrandt.com/

[70] https://www.cambridgeconsultants.com/press-releases/turning-our-sketches-art-machine-learning

[71] Hernandez, C. and Flores, R. Plus and minus RNAs of peach latent mosaic viroid self-cleave in vitro via hammerhead
structures. Proc. Natl. Acad. Sci, 1992.

[72] With reference to string theory.

[73] Douglas R. Hofstadter, Gödel, Escher, Bach: An Eternal Golden Braid, 1979.

[74] Catherine Voison, Contemporary art through the prism of biotechnologies, 2014.

[75] Meghana N. Thorat, Syed G. Dastager, High yield production of cellulose by a Komagataeibacter rhaeticus PG2 strain isolated from pomegranate as a new host, 2018.

[76] Samantha Michaels, A Conversation With Suzanne Lee, Sustainable Fashion Innovator, 2011.

[77] Victor Hugo, Les contemplations, 1856.

[78] Christian Bök, The Xenotext, 2015.

[79] Ovid, Metamorphoses (book X): Orphée et Eurydice, 8 ap. J.-C.

[80] Gustafsson, C. For anyone who ever said there's no such thing as a poetic gene. Nature, 458, 703, 2009.

[81] David Farrier, Anthropocene Poetics: Deep Time, Sacrifice Zones, and Extinction, 2019.

[82] Cox, M., Rising from the Ashes: DNA Repair in Deinococcus radiodurans, 2010.

[83] Cox, M., Battista, J. Deinococcus radiodurans - the consummate survivor. Nature Reviews Microbiology, 3, 882–892, 2005.

[84] Zala, K. Q&A: Poetry in the genes. Nature, 458 (7234), 35–35, 2009.

[85] With reference to CRISPR called the so-called genetic scissors technique.

[86] René Descartes, Discourse on Method, 1637.

[87] Grooten, M. and Almond, WWF. 2018. Living Planet Report, Let's be ambitious. REA WWF, Gland, Switzerland, 2018.

[88] Michel Serres, The natural contract, Le Pommier, 1990.

[89] For example Mount Mabu in Mozambique.

[90] www.planet.fr/dossiers-de-la-redaction-eggypt-17-nouvelles-pyramides-decouvertes-par-un-satellite-de-la-nasa.74482.1466.html

[91] Epelde, G., Morgan, F., Mujika, A., Callaly, F., Leškovský, P., McGinley, B., et al. Web-Based Interfaces for Virtual C. elegans Neuron Model Definition, Network Configuration, Behavioral Experiment Definition and Experiment Results Visualization. Frontiers in Neuroinformatics, 12, 80, 2018.

[92] Lüttge, U., & Souza, GM The Golden Section and beauty in nature: The perfection of symmetry and the charm of asymmetry. Progress in Biophysics and Molecular Biology, 146, 98–103, 2019.

[93] Fernando Corbalan, Etienne Ghys, Cédric Villani, The golden ratio : The mathematical language of beauty, 2013. Book series " The world is mathematical " is directed by the famous Cédric Villani describes a set of mathematical mysteries for better understand the world around us.

[94] S. Douady and Y. Couder, Phyllotaxis as a physical self-organized growth process, Phys. Rev. Lett. 68, 2098, 1992.

[95] Rafael J. Tamargo, Jonathan A. Pindrik. Mammalian Skull Dimensions and the Golden Ratio (Φ). Journal of Craniofacial Surgery; 30 (6), 2019.

[96] Luc Ferry, Biological nature is anything but a moral and political norm, Le Figaro, Thursday, February 14, 2013.

[97] Frank Wilczek, A Beautiful Question, 2016.

[98] Hans Slabbekoorn, Ardie den Boer-Visser, Cities Change the Songs of Birds, Current Biology, Volume 16, Issue 23, 2006.

[99] C. Chappuis, An example of the influence of the environment on the vocal emissions of birds: The evolution of songs in the equatorial forest, Terre Vie, 118, pp. 183-202, 1971.

[100] David, A. New Definitions of Humanism. In Progress in Biocybernetics, 1966.

[101] According to history, the II nd century AD, a bishop of St. Denis name was beheaded by order of the Roman power. A "miracle" then occurs: the tortured takes his head in his hands and begins to walk.

[102] Big data in the service of the Sustainable Development Goals https://www.un.org/en/sections/issues-depth/big-data-sustainable-development/index.html

[103] This involves studying the operating mode of a system in order to try to reproduce its operation.

[104] Petrushin, Alexey & Ferrara, Lorenzo & Blau, Axel. The Si elegans project at the interface of experimental and computational Caenorhabditis elegans neurobiology and behavior. Journal of Neural Engineering. 13, 2016.

[105] Cyborg Beetles, Michel M. Maharbiz and Hirotaka Sato, Scientific American, 303 (6), pp. 94-99, Published by: Scientific American, a division of Nature America, Inc, 2010.

[106] https://youtu.be/enA4MZrKqds

[107] Donna Haraway, " A Cyborg Manifesto: Science, Technology, and Socialist-Feminism in the Late Twentieth Century ", in Simians, Cyborgs and Women: The Reinvention of Nature, New York, Routledge, 1991.

[108] Hayles, N. Katherine, Reading and thinking in digital environments: Attention, stories, technogenesis, Christophe Degoutin (transl.), Grenoble : ELLUG, 2016.

[109] Quote from William James Durant.

[110] Llewellyn, D., Ding, Y., Faruque, II, Paesani, S., Bacco, D., Santagati, R., et al. Chip-to-chip quantum teleportation and multi-photon entanglement in silicon. Nature Physics, 16 (2), 148–153, 2019.

[111] R. Alexander Bentley, Michael J. O'Brien, The Acceleration of Cultural Change, From Ancestors to Algorithms, 2017.

[112] Michel Desmurget, La fabrique du crétin digital, 2019.

[113] Yuval Noah Harari, Homo Deus: A Brief History of the Future, 2015.

[114] Foldit is developed by a collaboration of the University of Washington Center for Game Science, the University of Washington Institute for Protein Design, Northeastern University, Vanderbilt University, the University of California, Davis and the 'University of Massachusetts, Dartmouth, https://fold.it.

[115] François Jacob, The Game of Possibilities: Essay on the Diversity of Living Things, Fayard, 1981.

[116] Venter, J. Craig, Life at the Speed of Light: From the Double Helix to the Dawn of Digital Life, 2013.

[117] Louis Aragon, The eyes of Elsa, Seghers: Poetry first, 1942.

[118] https://bioviva-science.com

[119] Dara Mohammadi and Nicola Davis, Can this woman cure aging with gene therapy?, 2016.

[120] Shanna Rajpar, Lionel Guittat, Jean-Louis Mergny, Telomeres: a Nobel for the beginning of the end, Bulletin du Cancer, Volume 98, Issue 9, 2011.

[121] With the emergence of cryptocurrencies and the risk of theft, some citizens have had an RFID chip implanted with the private key allowing access to their virtual wallet.

[122] https://www.2-sight.com/ System prosthesis Retinal Argus ®

[123] Epicure, Letter to Ménécée, Translation by Octave Hamelin, Electronic edition: Les Échos du Maquis, 2011.

[124] William Shakespeare, Hamlet, 1601.

[125] Baar, Marjolein & Brandt, Renata & Putavet et al. Targeted Apoptosis of Senescent Cells Restores Tissue Homeostasis in Response to Chemotoxicity and Aging. Cell. 169. 2017.

[126] Lujambio, A. To clear, or not to clear (senescent cells)? That is the question. BioEssays 38, S56 – S64, 2016.

[127] George M. Church, Regenesis: How Synthetic Biology Will Reinvent Nature and Ourselves, Kindle Edition, Ed Regis, 2012.

[128] Rothemund, Paul WK Folding DNA to create nanoscale shapes and patterns, Nature 440: 297-302, 2006.

[129] DNA origami applications in cancer therapy Anuttara Udomprasert and Thaned Kangsamaksin, Cancer Sci. Aug; 108 (8): 1535–1543, 2017.

[130] Andrew V. Anzalone, Peyton B. Randolph et al., Sear ch-and-replace genome editing without double-strand breaks or donor DNA, Nature, 2019.

[131] Verdin E. NAD $^+$ in aging, metabolism, and neurodegeneration. Science ; 350 (6265), 2015.

[132] Size of the anti-aging market worldwide from 2018 to 2023, Statista, 2018.

[133] Annabelle Laurent, Talking to the dead will be, in the future, as natural as opening Facebook ", 20 minutes, 2016.

[134] Initiative on the occasion of the launch of the last season of the Versailles series, INfluencia, 2018.

[135] Baars, Bernard & Franklin, Stan. Consciousness is computational: The LIDA model of global workspace theory. International Journal of Machine Consciousness, 2009.

[136] Shen, G., Horikawa, T., Majima, K., & Kamitani, Y. Deep image reconstruction from human brain activity. PLoS Computational Biology, 15 (1), 1–23, 2019.

[137] Capogrosso, M., Milekovic, T., Borton, D. et al. A brain – spine interface alleviating gait deficits after spinal cord injury in primates. Nature 539, 284–288, 2016.

[138] Velliste, M., Perel, S., Spalding, M. et al. Cortical control of a prosthetic arm for self-feeding. Nature 453, 1098–1101, 2008.

[139] Rao RPN, Stocco A, Bryan M, Sarma D, Youngquist TM, Wu J, et al. A Direct Brain-to-Brain Interface in Humans, 2014.

[140] Jiang, Linxing & Stocco, Andrea & Losey, Darby & Abernethy, Justin & Prat, Chantel & Rao, Rajesh. BrainNet: A Multi-Person Brain-to-Brain Interface for Direct Collaboration Between Brains. Scientific Reports, 2019.

[141] Action potentials travel through the axons of neurons to allow the release of neurotransmitters.

[142] Markram H †, Muller E †, Ramaswamy S †, Reimann MW †, Abdellah M, Sanchez CA, Ailamaki A, Alonso-Nanclares L, Antille N, Arsever S et al. Reconstruction and Simulation of Neocortical Microcircuitry. Cell 163: 2, 456 - 492, 2015.

[143] Human Brain Project: 1.19 billion euros for a CERN of the brain, Laurent Sacco, 2013.

[144] Neuron-specific signatures in the chromosomal connectome associated with schizophrenia risk, Prashanth Rajarajan, Tyler Borrman, et al., Science, 2018.

[145] Demarse TB, Wagenaar DA, Blau AW, Potter SM. The Neurally Controlled Animat: Biological Brains Acting with Simulated Bodies. Auton Robots; 11 (3), 2001.

[146] Using Sinusoidally-Modulated Noise as a Surrogate for Slow-Wave Sleep to Accomplish Stable Unsupervised Dictionary Learning in a Spike-Based Sparse Coding Model, CVPR Women in Computer Vision Workshop, 2020.

[147] http://www.2045.com

[148] Oscar Wilde's original formulation is: " We are all in the gutter, but some of us are looking at the stars. "

[149] Isaac Asimov, The cycle of robots, Volume 1, The robots, 1950.

[150] Peter Kramer, Prozac, prescription happiness? - A doctor's investigation into new treatments for depression, 1994.

[151] Ray Kurzweil, Human Body Version 2.0, 2003.

[152] Alcor Life Extension Foundation, https://alcor.org

[153] J. Folch et al., First birth of an animal from an extinct subspecies (Capra pyrenaica pyrenaica) by cloning, Theriogenology, vol. 71, n º 6, 2009.